EXTRAORDINARY
INDIANS

Also by Khushwant Singh

FICTION
Train to Pakistan
I Shall Not Hear the Nightingale
Delhi: A Novel
The Company of Women
Burial at Sea
The Sunset Club
The Portrait of a Lady: Collected Stories

NON-FICTION
Truth, Love & a Little Malice: An Autobiography
Delhi Through the Seasons
Indira Gandhi Returns
A History of the Sikhs
Ranjit Singh: Maharaja of the Punjab

ANTHOLOGIES
The Freethinker's Prayer Book
Unforgettable Khushwant Singh: His Finest Fiction, Non-fiction, Poetry & Humour
Portrait of a Serial Killer: Uncollected Writings
Me, the Jokerman: Enthusiasms, Rants & Obsessions

TRANSLATIONS
Land of Five Rivers
Umrao Jan Ada (with M. A. Husaini)
Shikwa and Jawab-i-Shikwa
Celebrating the Best of Urdu Poetry (with Kamna Prasad)

EXTRAORDINARY
INDIANS
A BOOK OF PROFILES

KHUSHWANT SINGH

edited by Mala Dayal

ALEPH

ALEPH

ALEPH BOOK COMPANY
An independent publishing firm
promoted by *Rupa Publications India*

First published in India in 2017
by Aleph Book Company
7/16 Ansari Road, Daryaganj
New Delhi 110 002

Copyright © Mala Dayal 2017
Introduction © Mala Dayal 2017
The Acknowledgements (on Page 205) are an extension of
the copyright page.

Cover images courtesy Wikimedia Commons
Mother Teresa: © 1986 Túrelio (via Wikimedia-Commons),
1986/Lizenz: Creative Commons CC-BY-SA-2.0 de
A. P. J. Abdul Kalam: Wikimedia-Commons/DwWorkStudio
Photography
Indira Gandhi: Wikimedia-Commons/Warren K. Leffler

All rights reserved.

The views and opinions expressed in this book are the
author's own and the facts are as reported by him, which have
been verified to the extent possible, and the publishers are not
in any way liable for the same.

While every effort has been made to trace copyright holders
and obtain permission, this has not been possible in all cases;
any omissions brought to our attention will be remedied in
future editions.

No part of this publication may be reproduced, transmitted,
or stored in a retrieval system, in any form or by any means,
without permission in writing from Aleph Book Company.

ISBN: 978-93-83064-73-1

1 3 5 7 9 10 8 6 4 2

Printed and bound in India by Replika Press Pvt. Ltd.

This book is sold subject to the condition that it shall not,
by way of trade or otherwise, be lent, resold, hired out, or
otherwise circulated without the publisher's prior consent in
any form of binding or cover other than that in which it is
published.

CONTENTS

Introduction   vii

POLITICIANS

1. Pandit Nehru — 3
2. Mahatma Gandhi — 6
3. Maulana Azad — 9
4. Indira Gandhi — 16
5. Rajiv Gandhi — 26
6. V. P. Singh — 29
7. Giani Zail Singh — 41
8. Dr A. P. J. Abdul Kalam — 47
9. Jayaprakash Narayan — 50

SPIRITUAL LEADERS

10. Acharya Rajneesh — 63
11. U. G. Krishnamurti — 67
12. Guru Nanak — 70
13. Mother Teresa — 72
14. Kabir — 77
15. Bhai Vir Singh — 80
16. Dadaji — 85

WRITERS/ARTISTS

17. Dhiren Bhagat — 89
18. R. K. Narayan — 91
19. Ali Sardar Jafri — 93
20. Firaq Gorakhpuri — 96
21. Nirad C. Chaudhuri — 98
22. Mulk Raj Anand — 102
23. Qurratulain Hyder — 105
24. Nirala — 108

25. Ghalib	111
26. Mir Taqi Mir	114
27. Dom Moraes	118
28. Amir Khusrau	121
29. R. K. Laxman	127
30. V. S. Naipaul	129
31. Faiz Ahmed Faiz	132

FAMILY AND FRIENDS

32. Daadimaa	139
33. Sobha Singh	143
34. Veeran Bai	146
35. Rajni Patel	149
36. Dharma Kumar	151
37. Aveek Sarkar	155
38. Prabha Dutt	158
39. P. C. Lal	161
40. Manzur Qadir	163

OTHERS

41. Hardayal	169
42. J. R. D. Tata	172
43. G. D. Birla	174
44. Nargis Dutt	176
45. Protima Bedi	179
46. Chetan Anand	182
47. Ranjit Singh	185
48. KS on KS	187

AND TWO WHO FLATTERED TO DECEIVE

49. Lal Krishna Advani	199
50. Sanjay Gandhi	202

Acknowledgements	205

INTRODUCTION

'The juggernaut of Hindu fundamentalism has emerged from the temple of intolerance and is on its yatra. Whoever stands in its way will be crushed under its mighty wheels.' These anguished words of my father reflected his anger and depression. If he were alive today, his distress would have deepened. He would have fought, in his inimitable way, the corrupt in politics and out of it; he would have stood up against the communal forces that are destroying the pluralism of India today. One of the unfortunate consequences of the rise of the right wing is the sanctification of men with feet of clay and villainous figures of history. This would have made my father very unhappy, as all his life he did not hesitate to excoriate crooked politicians and religious fundamentalists of every faith.

This collection of fifty profiles, published to commemorate the seventieth anniversary of India's Independence, is a small attempt to restore the balance. It comprises sketches of Indians who were truly extraordinary, not false heroes and saints. I have also included a sketch of an extraordinary Pakistani, my father's closest and most-admired friend. There are portraits of politicians and spiritual leaders, industrialists and movie stars, writers and artists. The historical figure Maharaja Ranjit Singh also finds a place, as do my father's grandmother, parents and some friends—some well known, others less so. Most were people my father had met and interacted with. As a counterpoint, there are profiles of two people who flattered to deceive, L. K. Advani, and Sanjay Gandhi, whose espousal brought my father much criticism. To round off the collection there are two charming pieces on himself.

A glaring omission in the book is the absence of a profile of my mother. My father and mother had known each other since their school days in Modern School. Though Modern School was co-educational, very few parents chose to send their daughters there. My mother often related an incident about their childhood: On a Founder's Day, the children played many games, including 'hiding the presents'. Because she was considered a tomboy, her present was hidden in the topmost branch of a tree. My father told her where her present was, got her a ladder and helped her climb the tree. As soon as she reached the branch, he removed the ladder. She yelled and screamed, and a crowd gathered. The ladder was put up again, and she came down abusing my father. After school, she was one of the few women to join St. Stephen's College, Delhi. Thereafter, she went to England to train as a Montessori teacher. She was no longer a tomboy, and had grown into a much sought-after, beautiful young woman. My father was obviously bowled over.

My father would not have been the person he was without my mother in his life. She supported him in whatever he chose to do, brought him back to earth whenever he got rather pleased with himself—which he acknowledged in his writing.

This book is dedicated to the memory of my mother (1916-2001).

Mala Dayal
New Delhi
June 2017

POLITICIANS

PANDIT NEHRU
(1889–1964)

Pandit Jawaharlal Nehru, it must be said, fully answered the poet Allama Iqbal's requirements of a Meer-e-Kaarvaan—leader of the caravan:

> *Nigah buland, sukhan dilnawaz, jaan par soz*
> *Yahi hain rakht-e-safar Meer-e-Kaarvaan ke liye*
>
> Lofty vision, winning speech and a warm personality
> This is all the baggage the leader of a caravan needs on his journey

Nehru should have been the role model for the prime ministers of India. He was above prejudices of any kind: racial, religious or of caste. He was an agnostic and firmly believed that religion played a very negative role in Indian society. What I admired most about him was his secularism. He was a visionary and an exemplary leader; the father of Indian constitutional democracy; of universal adult franchise; the five-year plans and giving equal rights to women, among other things. He was better educated than any of his successors, with the exception of Manmohan Singh, and spent nine long years in jail reading, writing and thinking about the country's future.

But being human, Nehru had his human failings. He was not above political chicanery. Having accepted the Cabinet Mission Plan to hand over power to a united India, he reneged on his undertaking when he realized that M. A. Jinnah might end up becoming prime minister. Nehru had blind spots too. He refused to believe that India's exploding population needed to be contained. He refused to see the gathering strength of Muslim separatism that led to the formation of Pakistan. He failed to come to terms with Pakistan and was chiefly responsible for the mess we made in Jammu and Kashmir. He was also given to nepotism and favouritism. And his love affairs with Shraddha Mata and Lady Edwina Mountbatten are well known.

I first met Nehru in London, when I was a press officer at

the Indian Embassy. Senior members of staff at the embassy were ordered to be present at Heathrow to receive the Prime Minister. It was a cold winter night when the plane touched down. 'What are all of you doing here at this unearthly hour?' he demanded, obviously expecting us to be present and pleased to note that we were discharging our duties. Menon asked me to introduce myself to the PM and ask him if he desired me to do anything. I did so only to be snubbed. 'What would I want of you at this hour? Go home and get some sleep.'

He could also be ill-mannered. I once had to host a lunch so that the editors of leading British newspapers could meet him. Halfway through the meal, Nehru fell silent. When questions were put to him, he looked up at the ceiling and did not reply. He then proceeded to light a cigarette while others were still eating. To make matters worse, Krishna Menon fell asleep. It was a disastrous attempt at public relations.

Another time, Nehru arrived in London past midnight. I asked him whether he would like me to accompany him to his hotel. 'Don't be silly,' he said. 'Go home and sleep.' The next morning, one of the papers carried a photo of him with Lady Mountbatten opening the door in her negligee. The photographer had taken the chance of catching them, if not in flagrante delicto, at least in preparation of it, and got his scoop. The huge caption read: 'Lady Mountbatten's Midnight Visitor'. Nehru was furious. On another occasion, he had taken Lady Mountbatten for a quiet dinner at a Greek restaurant. Once again, the following morning's papers carried photographs of them sitting close to each other. Our prime minister's liaison with Lady Edwina had assumed scandalous proportions, and I knew I was in trouble.

I arrived at the office to find a note from Krishna Menon on my table, saying that the Prime Minister wished to see me immediately.

I gently knocked on the Prime Minister's door and went in. He was busy going through some files.

'Yes?' he said, raising his head.

'Sir, you sent for me. '

'I sent for you? Who are you?'

'I am your PRO (public relations officer) in London, sir,' I replied.

He looked me up and down. 'You have a strange notion of publicity,' he said curtly.

I thought it best to remain silent.

MAHATMA GANDHI
(1869–1948)

In the study in my cottage in Kasauli, I have pictures of the people I admire most—one of them is Mahatma Gandhi. I admire Bapu Gandhi more than any other man. Of all the other prophets of the past we have no knowledge. Almost everything about them is myth or miracle. With Gandhi, we know—he walked among us not long ago and there are many people alive, like me, who have seen him. He was always in the public eye. He bared himself; no one was more honest.

I don't accept his foibles. He took a vow of celibacy in his prime, but without consulting his wife, which I think was grossly unfair. He would sleep naked beside young girls to test his brahmacharya. He could be very odd. But his insistence on truth at all times made him a Mahatma. And the principle of ahimsa: not to hurt anyone. Ahimsa and honesty should be the basis of all religion, of every life.

I have been a regular drinker all my adult life. I celebrate sex and cannot say that I have never lied. I have not hurt anyone physically, but I think I have caused hurt with my words and actions. And sometimes there is no forgiveness in me. But I consider myself a Gandhian. Whenever I feel unsure of anything, I try to imagine what Gandhi would have done, and that is what I do.

If only Mahatma Gandhi were alive today, the situation of the country would have been different. I don't believe the likes of Anna Hazare can do a thing about corruption in India—his fasting is to no avail. Only Mahatma Gandhi would have been able to arouse mass consciousness to halt the tide of corruption and chaos spreading around us today.

I became a Gandhi bhakt at a young age. I first saw Bapu when I was six or seven years old, when I was studying at Modern School. He had come on a visit. All of us children—there were very few students in the school in those days—sat on the ground in the front row. Bapu bent down and tugged my uniform playfully.

'Beta, yeh kapda kahaan ka hai?' he asked. (Where is this cloth from?)

'Vilayati,' I said with pride. (It is from abroad.)

He told me gently, 'Yeh apne desh ka hota toh acchha hota, nahin?' (It would have been good had this been from our country, wouldn't it?)

Soon after, I started wearing khadi. My mother used to spin khaddar, so it was easy. I continued wearing khaddar for many years. Before I went to London to attend university, I took some khaddar to our tailor because I had been told I would need a proper English suit. The tailor laughed and told my father, who asked me to stop being a khotta (donkey).

Mahatma Gandhi was the one person who seemed to comprehend the grave consequences of the partition. He did not take part in any of the Independence celebrations. When anti-Pakistan feelings were at fever pitch and the Indian government refused to honour its pledge to pay Pakistan ₹55 crores, the Mahatma went on a fast and forced the government to abide by its word. He knew he was asking for trouble but did not give it a second thought. A calumny was spread about his having agreed to the partition of India along communal lines. He told his secretary Pyarelal: 'Today I find myself alone. Even the Sardar [Patel] and Jawaharlal Nehru think that my reading of the situation is wrong and peace is sure to return if the partition is agreed upon... I shall perhaps not be alive to witness it, but should the evil I apprehend overtake India and her independence be imperilled, let it not be said that Gandhi was party to India's vivisection.'

I was in London when Mahatma Gandhi was assassinated in Delhi on 30 January 1948. I had taken leave to pack my belongings to proceed to Canada. My wife and I had been invited to lunch by Sir Malcolm Darling, a retired income tax commissioner who lived in a basement flat near Victoria station. As we came out into the cold windy day after lunch, I noted scribbled in hand on a placard by a newspaper stall the message: 'Gandhi assassinated'. I did not believe it could be our Bapu. Who could kill a saintly man who had harmed no one? I asked the stall holder. He had tears in his eyes as he handed me a copy of the *Evening Standard*. 'Yes, mate, some bloody villain's got him,' he said. Tears also welled up in my eyes. I was only able to read the headlines. Instead of going on to the shipping office to confirm our passage, we made our way to India House to be with our people. Oil lamps had been lit at the base of Gandhi's portrait. The smell of aromatic incense pervaded the place. Men and women sat on the floor chanting Gandhi's favourite hymns. 'Vaishnav jan toh tainey kaheeye jo peed paraie jaane rey'—Know him only as a man of God who feels the suffering of others; and 'Ishwar Allah terey naam, sab ko sanmati dey Bhagwan'—Ishwar and Allah are but names of the same God, may His blessings be on us.

Bapu was pretty certain that he would not be allowed to live. At a prayer meeting on 16 June 1947, he had said, 'I shall consider myself brave if I am killed and if I still pray to God for my assassin.' As he had anticipated, the assassin finally got him the following year. He went with the name of Ram on his lips—a glorious end to a glorious life.

MAULANA AZAD
(1888–1958)

In the wake of Partition in August 1947, when millions of Muslims were compelled to leave their homes and properties to migrate to Pakistan, thousands had been butchered in the Hindu-Sikh versus Muslim riots and many were forced to seek shelter in refugee camps. Maulana Abul Kalam Azad, who had foreseen the consequences of dividing India on religious lines, addressed a vast throng of disillusioned Muslims of Delhi from the steps of Jama Masjid. He admonished them for not heeding the words of warning he had been speaking and writing his entire life. He said, 'You may not remember that I told you about all this to come but you sliced away my tongue; when I picked up my pen you cut off my hands; when I tried to lead you along the right path, you broke my legs; when I tried to turn, you broke my back.'

From the time Azad started his journalistic and political career in Calcutta in 1912 his message to his fellow Muslims was consistently the same. He chided them for keeping away from the freedom movement and letting non-Muslims be in the forefront of the liberation struggle. While Mohammad Ali Jinnah dubbed him 'The Show-boy of the Congress' and the vast majority of Indian Muslims supported the Muslim League's demand for a separate Muslim state, the Maulana remained a stolid supporter of the Indian National Congress. When Gandhi (reluctantly), Pandit Nehru and Sardar Patel acquiesced to the partition of the country, Azad stood alone among the leaders in opposing it. Where did he derive his strength to tread the lonely path, the courage to maintain that he was right and the others wrong? Without doubt his inspiration came from only one source, the Quran.

Azad was born in Makkah of an Indian father and an Arab mother. His first language was the language of the Quran, Arabic. His father came from a line of Islamic theologians and he was expected to continue in the profession. The family migrated back to Calcutta where Azad picked up Urdu and Persian. He went through a short phase of agnosticism, rejecting all faiths and apparently indulged himself in the pleasures of the flesh. Then he went back to Islam and from the very start of his career was convinced that it was the duty of Indian Muslims to join Hindus in the struggle for freedom. While still in his early twenties he started to publish an Urdu weekly, *Al-Hilal*. It rapidly picked up circulation, touching a figure of 29,000 (no mean figure for an Urdu journal in those days). Although he wrote mostly on religious topics, his nationalist views displeased the government, so the paper was banned. Azad launched another one, *Al Balagha*. It was in an issue of *Al Balagha* in 1916 that he announced that he had embarked on an Urdu translation of the Quran and had already rendered the first three chapters up to Surah Al-Imran, and hoped to finish the entire book by the end of the year.

That was not to be. On 3 March 1916, an order under the Defence of India Act compelled him to quit Calcutta. Most provincial governments refused him entry. His only choices were Bombay Presidency or Bihar. He chose Bihar because it was nearer to Calcutta and took up residence at Ranchi. He completed the translation of another chapter, Surah An-Nisa, where an order of internment was passed against him and all his papers seized. He appealed to the governor, Lord Sinha. After a fortnight, his papers were returned to him. This roused the ire of Sir Charles Cleveland, head of the CID, who travelled all the way from Delhi to Ranchi and re-seized the papers to have them scrutinized lest they contain inflammatory stuff. Hoping to have the papers returned to him, Azad went ahead with his translations and commentaries and completed the work in 1918. On his release he asked for his papers to be returned to him. After a long time they were, but before he could put them together he was re-arrested in November 1921 when the Indian National Congress was declared unlawful. For the third time his papers were seized and stuffed in gunny bags to be taken away. He was released after fifteen months in jail. His papers returned to him were torn, jumbled up and many pages destroyed. The Maulana lost heart and gave up the project as being ill-starred.

Five years later in 1927 he began all over again. He finished the translations and commentaries on 20 July 1930 while in detention in

Meerut jail. The genesis of three volumes of *The Tarjuman-ul Quran* (Translation of the Quran) shows the mettle of Maulana Azad.

One may well ask, why this passion to translate a book which had been translated several times into Urdu, English and most world languages? Azad was convinced that existing translations had missed the message of the Quran by introducing esoteric meanings to words which were simple, clear, so that illiterate Arab tribesmen could understand them. This happened after the Prophet's generation had died out and Islam had spread to non-Arab people. Greek, Iranian and Buddhist concepts found their way into interpreting the Quran. Personal views of commentators distorted meanings of simple Arabic words. Then there were the Sufis who looked for 'hidden meanings' when there was nothing hidden in the Quran. A verse states explicitly that the Quran was 'a light gleaming before the men and in their right hand'. The revelations did not claim to be the basis of a new faith but a reminder of the faith proclaimed by prophets like Abraham, Moses and Jesus Christ. 'This is no new tale of fiction,' claims the Quran 'but a confirmation of previous scriptures, an explanation of all things, and a guidance and mercy to those who believe.' Azad's motive was to 'explain the Quran in the manner of the Quran. He rarely goes beyond explaining the etymology of the words used and was very sparing in quoting translations ascribed to the Prophet (Hadith) to shore up his arguments.

Although young in years and with scant knowledge of European languages, Azad read extensively on whatever he could find on religion or philosophy that was available to him. Inevitably the influence of Muslim theologians weighed heavily on him. Foremost was Imam Ghazali (twelfth century) who, like him, had passed through a period of disbelief before returning to religion. Ghazali turned to mysticism; Azad, who had a Sufi background, rejected mysticism. Nevertheless, he admired some Sufis like the dervish Sarmad, who was condemned as a heretic by the ulema and beheaded under the order of Emperor Aurangzeb. Sarmad's green tomb is on the eastern end of the steps of Delhi's Jama Masjid, close to where Maulana Azad is buried. Of Sarmad he said: 'He stood on the minaret of love from which the walls of the kaaba and the temple appeared of equal height.'

It is interesting to note that Azad's contemporary, the poet Allama Iqbal, who was as deeply concerned with the future of his community, and like Azad drew his inspiration from Islamic sources, took a completely different path. Between 1905 and 1910, both travelled abroad. Iqbal went to Europe and was deeply impressed with the vitality of Western civilization and became more conscious of the decadence that had overtaken the Islamic world. He gave expression to it in his famous poem, *Shikwa* (Complaint). Although addressed to Allah, he wrote of the glorious past of the idol-breaking conquerors fired with zeal. Azad travelled to Muslim countries struggling for freedom from European colonial powers and felt that the only hope was to revive Islam by firing the Muslims with the spirit that Allah had bequeathed to the Prophet through his revelations: the Quran. Iqbal was inspired by Islamic history; Azad by the Quran and the life of the Prophet. Iqbal came to the conclusion that Muslims were a people apart from the Hindus and their salvation lay in a state of their own. Azad totally rejected the two-nation theory and the concept of a separate Muslim state as against the teachings of the Quran.

Of the three-volume translations of the Quran, the first, which deals with the opening Surah Al-Fatiha, is the most significant. It consists of a bare seven lines of a few words each:

> In the name of Allah, the Compassionate, the Merciful
> Praise is for Allah only, the Lord of all Being
> The Benevolent, the Merciful
> Master of the Day of Recompense
> Thee only do we serve and thee alone do we ask for help,
> Direct us to the straight path
> The path of those to whom thou hast been gracious
> Not of those to who have incurred thy displeasure, nor of those who have gone astray.

This chapter has been described as the core or essence of the Quran, the sufficient and the treasure house. Since it is the most repeated part of the Quran, one of the revelations confirms: 'O Prophet! It is a fact that we have given you these seven oft repeated verses and the great Quran. The Prophet himself acknowledged that it is 'the greatest of the three chapters' and 'there is no chapter to compare with it'.

The Prophet never laid claims to propounding a new religion but bringing back a people who had strayed from this straight path of worshipping God into animism, ancestor worship, totemism and idolatry. The two most commonly used names of God, Allah and Rabh, were both pre-Islamic. Allah is really an exclamation of wonder at the universe and its creator: 'Hail God'. The Sikhs' Wahe Guru is exactly the same. Rabh is a portmanteau word meaning the provider (Al Razzaq) as well as teacher, master and Lord. The Quran begins with hamd (praise) to Allah (Bismillah) and his two great qualities, benevolence (Al Rahman) and mercy (Al Rahim). Thereafter it emphasizes his qualities as the provider—Sustainer of the universe (Rabbul Alamin).

Maulana Azad points out that the things most needed in life—air, water and earth (to provide food)—are free gifts of God given in abundance. The Quran emphasizes this: 'And we send down water from the heavens in its due degree, and cause it to settle on the earth, and we have power for its withdrawal too, and by it, we cause gardens of palm trees and vineyards to spring forth for you, in which you have plenteous fruits and whereof you eat.'

Azad points out the difference between the Hindu and Islamic verses in the purpose of creation. Hindus believe that the universe is God's leela (sport) and unreal. Islam attributes deliberate purpose to creation. Says the Quran: 'We have not created the heavens and the earth and whatever is between them in sport: we have not created them but for a serious end.' Azad produces a telling argument for the existence of God. The nature of man can hardly believe that there can be an action without an actor, orderliness without a director, a plan without a planner, a building without a builder, a design without a designer.

Proof of God's existence, says Azad, is there for everyone who cares to see it and quotes the Quran. 'Let man look at his food, it was He who first rained down copious rains, there cleft the earth with clefts, and caused the up-growth of the grain, and grapes and healing herbs, and fruits and herbage, for the service of yourselves and your cattle.'

One may as well ask, if God is all-powerful, just and merciful why do calamities like earthquakes, volcano eruptions and floods take such a heavy toll on innocent lives? The Quran answers that the good and useful survive—'as to the former it is quickly gone and as to which is useful, it remaineth on the earth'.

Truth, assures the Quran, will always triumph over falsehood. God is Al-Haqqah—The Truthful One. 'We will hurl the truth at falsehood and it shall smite it; and lo! it will vanish.' The retribution for falsehood and evil need not be sudden because people are given time for repentance. 'I am with those who wait,' says the Quran. The time for repentance should not be frittered away. Repentance releases forces of mercy; every tear shed in contrition washes away the stains of sin. The Prophet himself gave assurance that 'one who repents sincerely is like one who never committed sin'. Azad followed up with the exhortation: 'What right have we to expect forgiveness from God when we have not learned to forgive our fellow creatures?'

It should be noted that, unlike Christianity, Islam does not ask people to love their enemies (which is contrary to nature) but only to forgive them. Hate the sin and not the sinner. It also justifies retaliation but limits it to the damage suffered. Contrary to popular notion, the Quran does not exhort Muslims to wage instant war against unbelievers (kafirs). It is only against those who persecute believers or revile the Quran and the Prophet that violence is sanctioned. Otherwise a person is free to believe what he or she thinks best. 'To you, your way, and to me, mine,' says the revelations and give the assurance: 'There is no compulsion in religion'.

An important attribute of God is Adalat—Justice; he is the master of the day of recompense. Maulana Azad emphasized that divine justice is not dependent on the whim of God but entirely based on the law of causation—what you sow, you reap.

Azad differs from other theologians in saying that the concept of one almighty God is not an evolutionary process but the revival of one with which the world started: 'Men were first of one religion only; then they fell to variance', says the Quran. Azad also believed that the Islamic concept of God is more advanced than the Jewish and the Christian because the Jews regarded Him as the tribal God of a 'chosen people' while the Christians humanized him as much as they regarded Jesus as the 'Son of God'. The Quran was close to the Upanishads in refusing to define God (neti, neti—not this, not this) but took a more positive attitude by making Him a repository of attributes—creativity, providence, justice, mercy and so on. The Prophet did his utmost to avoid being treated as an incarnation or avatar of Allah. When he died, his father-in-law, the first Caliph, spoke to the gathering: 'He who worshipped Muhammad, let them know that Muhammad is dead, and he who worshipped God, let him know that God ever lives. He has no death.' In emphasizing God as the sole object of worship, the Quran specifically forbade ascribing partners to share this singular sovereignty.

It is to this one rule of the universe that mankind must turn for guidance (Hidayat) to lead us along the straight path, the one trodden by the righteous, not evildoers.

It was his firm conviction in the unity of God and the brotherhood of mankind revealed in the Quran that made Maulana Azad turn his face against the concept of separate states based on religious differences. 'Whatever your so-called race, your homeland, your nationality, and whatever your circumstances in life or sphere of activity, if only you all resolve to serve but one God, all these will lose their sting. Your hearts will be united. You will begin to feel that the entire globe is your home and that all mankind is but one people, and that you all form but a single family—Ayaal Allah—the family of God.'

INDIRA GANDHI
(1917–1984)

Indira Gandhi has had more ups and downs in her sixty-three years than any other woman: her childhood and adolescence overshadowed by giants, her middle years blighted by insinuations that she had inherited a domain she did not deserve; then suddenly pedestalled to supreme heights, worshipped by the masses as a goddess reincarnated, execrated by the elite as the female incarnation of the devil and a fascist dictator. In a handful, she inspires dread, in the remaining millions she raises hope as the nation's redeemer. These are different facets of this one woman. Age has not withered her nor did custom stale her infinite variety.

Friends who are under the impression that I know Indira Gandhi well often ask me: 'What is she really like as a person?' My answer, based on scraps of information picked up from people who see her every day and from my own observations, runs somewhat as follows: She is very likeable if you are on her right side. Icily aloof if you are not. For those on her right side she can produce a smile which will dissolve a stone statue. For those who have incurred her displeasure she can be the reincarnation of Durga: few people have developed the technique of snubbing into as fine an art as she. An Indira-snub will rankle for years. And woe betide anyone who tries to appear familiar or spreads canards about being close to her. She is close to no one except herself. And next to herself she is closest to her younger son, Sanjay, only because they share a common interest in politics. The elder, Rajiv, does not share this interest and therefore sees less of her than his brother. Almost as if to compensate for the uneven distribution of closeness between her sons, she is closer to Rajiv's wife, Sonia, who has no interest in politics than to Sanjay's wife, Maneka, who is totally absorbed in it. She is inordinately fond of her grandchildren. Her seven-person family (an eighth is on the way) is as closely-knit as any traditional Hindu joint family. Whatever tensions they have are resolved without a whisper being heard outside. She sets no store by friendship and has therefore never bothered to cultivate any. She suffers expressions of friendship for what they are worth and is little perturbed when those who had protested their friendship turn against her. Her circle of acquaintances embraces the entire world.

Indira Gandhi has no set routine because she is hardly ever in the same place for more than a few days at a stretch. When she is in residence in Delhi, she rises well before dawn. Since she keeps her bedroom bolted from the inside, even members of the household do not know what she does in the first two hours of the morning. As her bedroom is crammed with books, it can be presumed she reads, writes letters and works on speeches she has to make that day. She is very punctilious about her health and spends fifteen to twenty minutes, morning and evening, doing yogic asanas. The secret of her physical vitality and freedom from tension in a tension-ridden life lies in the half-hour she spends in the care of her body. The newspapers are brought in with morning tea at 6 a.m. She does no more than scan the headlines. She has neither time nor patience to read magazines and has some kind of inhibition against reading anything about herself. She picks up news, comments and political gossip from the hundreds of people who see her every day. Very frequently she has one of her secretaries read out important clippings to her while she is working on her files. One thing she does not like to miss is arranging flowers brought in by the mali. Flower arrangement has always been her passion.

The family tries to be together at meals. This is not very easy as their daily schedules are as different as their culinary tastes. They manage to combine both at the breakfast table. Thereafter begin the day's hectic activities. By the time Indira Gandhi emerges on to the front veranda, a couple of hundred people who have been let in are scattered about the lawns and under the flowing chorisia tree facing the house. Several hundred others await their turn outside the gates. She receives a few in her sparsely furnished sitting room. It has a couple of sofas and four armchairs. One of these in a corner is designated as 'madam's chair'—no one else might sit in it. Above her head on the wall is a photograph of her father by Yousuf Karsh. A long glass-topped table bears a bowl of flowers and an ash tray. Presiding over the room from above the fireplace is a long, rectangular green and white painting of a young boy playing the flute with a dove perched on his shoulders. This is by the Mexican artist, Rafael Navarro. There is a smaller painting of Gandhiji and Tagore by Jamini Roy; two etchings in sepia: one of Amber Fort and the other of the tomb of Muhammad Tughlaq by an unknown English artist. It is in the same drawing room that her inner Cabinet of advisers and small delegations meet her. Between these confabulations she comes out to greet the assembled crowd, to be garlanded and photographed with them. On an average between 500 to 2,000 people have themselves photographed with her every day. She is said to have wistfully remarked: 'I have become one of the sights of Delhi.' In recent months, flower sellers, ice cream vendors and chaatwalas have established themselves outside 12, Willingdon Crescent, to cater to the crowds that come to see her.

'I have never met anyone who has this enormous capacity for work as Indiraji,' says R. K. Dhawan. 'After retiring at 3 a.m. she is up by six and in the office at eight attending to her files and correspondence. None of the chief ministers and governors who accompanied her on her state visits could stand the pace she set and were exhausted in a couple of days. Madam...never. After her visit they needed a few days off to recover. In the eighteen years I have been with her, I have never known her to complain of overwork. She once told me "tiredness is a state of mind; if you think you are tired, you get tired. If you don't think about it you never tire".'

Indira Gandhi drives herself to the utmost of her capacity, often doing two things at the same time. While she is reading a file she will get one of her secretaries to read out the news or brief her on a totally unrelated topic; her eyes scan the print, her ears take in the speech, her mind comprehends both. She is a great stickler for detail. Not only does she dot all the i's and cross all the t's in her speeches, when she goes abroad she prepares all the menus for the banquets she has to give to return the hospitality of her hosts.

Everyone who has seen her is struck by the neatness of her appearance and her excellent taste in clothes. She obviously takes great pains over her appearance. Her hair is well-coiffured, the distinct swathe of white which runs upwards from the middle of her forehead gives her a touch of the regal. Without having to wear a crown she looks every inch the Empress of India. She is at once the most simply and most elegantly dressed woman one can see anywhere. She wears no make-up or perfume and, apart from the rudraksha necklace, wears no jewellery of any kind. Her saris as well as her salwar kameez and shawls are made of coarse handspun cottons or silks available at the khadi bhandars. She chooses her own clothes and has her shirts and blouses stitched under her own supervision. Most of her saris are of light pastel shades. In any party of women gaudily attired in brocades and chiffons, dripping with gold and diamonds, Indira Gandhi stands out as the one dressed simply but in impeccable taste.

Unlike the common run of Indian politicians, Indira Gandhi rarely talks about herself or indulges in gossip about others. But she is not averse to listening to gossip as long as she is not brought into it. I recall once making an adverse remark about B. D. Jatti and asking her what made her choose such a nondescript character to be vice president of India. Her answer was a frozen stare. I never again took the liberty of soliciting her views on anyone. Her favourite pastime is to recount anecdotes of her early days with her parents and the celebrities she has met. She has few other interests. She has no time to indulge in music or go to dance recitals. She never watches television and only once or twice in the year goes to see a movie—an English, never a Hindi, movie.

Indira Gandhi provides very poor copy to journalists but can be a most rewarding person to have as a guest. Unlike most of her countrymen who see no discourtesy in keeping their hosts and other guests waiting for hours, Indira Gandhi will turn up on the expected minute. And unlike other important Indians who are totally absorbed in their own importance, Indira Gandhi is observant, will discuss children and clothes with women, speak words of appreciation to the cook and take care to talk to everyone in the party. She honoured my home on a few occasions to meet foreign correspondents posted in Delhi.

She missed nothing about my little apartment. I had lit oil lamps around the stone Ganapati at the entrance. She sensed this had been done in her honour. She examined it, asked how old it was and pronounced it beautiful. She went round the shelves looking at the books. She examined old maps on the walls (I have a collection of sixteenth-century maps of India) and all the paintings. A large photograph of the interior of the Madurai temple taken by my friend T. S. Nagarajan attracted her attention. 'That's a very good photograph,' she remarked. 'If you like good photographs I'll show you a better one in my study,' I said. In my study was the framed cover of an issue of the *Illustrated Weekly of India* with three faces of Indira Gandhi in different moods. A faint blush of a compliment accepted spread on her face. She made no comment but it obviously put her in a happy mood. Even when Peter Niesewand of *The Guardian* and Mark Tully of the BBC (who reminded her that she had had him expelled from India during the Emergency) tried to bait her, she refused to rise to their baits and remained cool and smiling.

I had gone to some trouble in getting a bottle of sherry as I had been told by a retired ambassador with whom she had stayed in Tokyo on an official visit that it was the only alcoholic drink that she took. 'Where on earth did you get the idea that I take sherry?' she demanded. I told her. 'Absolute rubbish! I have never touched any alcohol in my life. Since everyone offers it abroad at every party and if you say "I don't drink" they want to know why, I usually take a glass of sherry and keep it beside me throughout the party. It saves me from having to argue about it.'

The evening passed very pleasantly. Some of the correspondents were pretty rough with Sanjay. 'Do you want to become prime minister of India?' I heard someone ask him. He kept his cool and replied, 'I haven't given the prospect much thought.' After Indira Gandhi and Sanjay had left, the other guests stayed on, discussing the mother and son over coffee and cognac. 'She's charming! She's gracious! You can hardly believe she can cope with these ruffianly politicians she has to deal with!' were some of the comments they made. Even Sanjay came in for many compliments: 'He's all there! Heard so much against him, I couldn't believe this polite young fellow was the same man! But he has a hard streak in him...like someone who's been hurt.' And so on.

I also had occasion to see Indira Gandhi at several embassy receptions. She was invariably the greatest draw wherever she went. No sooner had the president or vice president been ushered in with the fanfare of national anthems, they were left to themselves and the guests swarmed around Indira Gandhi. Even if the ambassadors maintained diplomatic aloofness, their wives and children clustered round her to be photographed with her. At an iftar party at the Kuwait Embassy, the ambassador's young son insisted on shaking her by the hand. 'I want you to be prime minister of India again,' he said, gushing with enthusiasm.

'And why do you want me to be prime minister?' asked Indira Gandhi.

'Because I want to have my Coca Cola again!'

Another trait that marks Indira Gandhi as very different from other Indian politicians is that she measures every word she speaks. Experience has taught her never to commit herself in words which might be misconstrued when repeated. Even to a direct question her answer is never a straight 'Yes' or 'No'. Very often the answer is a blank stare that leaves one guessing. It is often alleged that she who is so astute in judging political situations, is a poor judge of people and is kaan ki kacchi—soft in the ear and influenced by gossip. There is little doubt that although she has the gift of passionate intuition about situations, it does not extend to an insight into human character. She is known to extend her patronage generously to people of little substance. She has often no better reason for doing so than a woman's reason: 'I think him so, because I think him so.'

It had so often mystified me how so many men and women, picked out of nowhere and put on the national stage, disowned her in times of crisis. The answer often given is that Indira Gandhi does not have the human warmth of the kind her father had; she is also said to be unusually suspicious of people's motives and therefore unable to command the sort of loyalty that held colleagues to Pandit Nehru despite his quick and explosive temper. R. K. Dhawan who has served both the father and the daughter has a different view: 'Nehru took the PM's chair when he was already a national hero. He could provide all the ambitious politicians and civil servants with jobs vacated by the British. Nehru also had no occasion to test the loyalties of these people because he never faced a real challenge to his leadership. It was different for Indira. By the time she took her father's place all the posts had been filled: the ambitions of ambitious men and women serving under her could not be fully realized. The sense of patriotism that had fired Nehru's generation had also vanished. Many of those that Indiraji raised to situations of importance either became frustrated because they could go no further or succumbed to temptations and had much to hide. Whenever Indiraji's position as a leader was questioned and they felt she might lose, they went over to what they felt was the winning side either to realize their unfulfilled ambitions or to get away with their misdeeds.' Dhawan is right. If you go over the list of ditchers and examine the circumstances in which they deserted her you will see that one of the two caps—unfulfilled ambition or corruption—fits their skulls.

They say Nehru was quick to temper and was sometimes unable to control his fits of rage. But these fits went as soon as they came and he never bore a grudge for too long. They say that Indira seldom loses her temper but once she is put off by a person she never forgives him or her. There is little truth to this. She seldom loses her cool and never raises her voice. What her father did with angry words she does with a deftly administered snub. But, like her father, she also does not harbour a grievance for too long. In her political work, which includes collections of funds for her party, she has always had to trust people with the job to act on her behalf. Many have in the process lined their own pockets. She has borne with them patiently and when convinced of their corruption, quietly relieved them of the task without any fanfare.

My hour of trial came when in May 1975 Mrs Gandhi imposed an Emergency on the country and arrested, among others, Jayaprakash Narayan, whom I admired. I had spent a few days with him and his wife during the famine in Bihar in 1967. However, I felt that his call for a Total Revolution, which involved gheraos of legislatures to prevent members elected by the people from discharging their duties, was a violation of a basic rule of democracy. I wrote to him saying so. He sent me a long reply defending his position. I published his letter in full. Conditions of anarchy had come to prevail. Every day there was a bandh of some kind; schools and colleges were closed for weeks in the affected parts of the country. Large processions marched through streets, smashing up shop windows and wrecking cars parked on the roads. Mrs Gandhi was driven to despair. Her position became vulnerable when the Allahabad High Court held her guilty of electoral malpractices and disqualified her from membership of Parliament. She was persuaded by her son Sanjay and advisers like Siddhartha Shankar Roy to suspend the Constitution, arrest members of the Opposition and muzzle the press.

I was at the time in Mexico and arrived back in Bombay on the morning after the declaration of the Emergency. I was dismayed. I was with members of the *Times of India* group who resolved not to give in to censorship imposed on us. Among those who refused to protest was Sham Lal, editor of the *Times of India*; among those who avoided making any commitment either way was Inder Malhotra. That evening my friend Rajni Patel, member of the board of directors of the *Times of India* and a confidante of Mrs Gandhi, rang me up and told me bluntly: 'My friend, if you are looking for martyrdom by going to jail, we will be happy to oblige you.' The chairman of the board, Justice K. T. Desai, counselled patience: 'Take your time. But if you refuse to publish we have to look for another editor,' he said.

My attitude to the Emergency was ambivalent. I supported the move to clamp down on law breakers (including Jayaprakash Narayan), but felt that censorship of the press would prove counter-productive as it would deprive editors like me, who supported Mrs Gandhi, of credibility. For three weeks I did not publish *The Weekly*, and when forced to resume publication gave instructions that no photographs of Mrs Gandhi or her ministers were to be used. I was treated gently, as I was regarded by Mrs Gandhi and Sanjay as a friend. I was summoned to Delhi to meet Mrs Gandhi. I protested against censorship imposed on people like me. I had my say. Before leaving I told her, 'My father was sure that if I spoke my mind, you would have me locked up.' She smiled and bade me goodbye. *The Weekly* was treated as a special case. I published articles by critics of the Emergency and pleaded for the release of political prisoners.

My meeting with Mrs Gandhi was meant to be secret. I arrived back in Bombay to find a letter on my table reading, 'How did your meeting with Madam Dictator go? George.' It was from George Fernandes who was then underground. A few days later four senior members of the RSS, against whom warrants of arrest had been issued, coolly walked into my office, had coffee with me, and asked me what had transpired at my meeting with the Prime Minister. I got the impression that the RSS was not against the Emergency and would be willing to cooperate with the government if its leaders were set at liberty.

For some weeks every article of *The Weekly* had to be cleared by the censor. They only bothered with politics and there wasn't much of that in my journal. The editor of *Debonair*, the Indian version of *Playboy*, told me that whenever he took his material for clearance, the censor would skip over stories and girlie pictures saying, 'Porn theek hai, politics nahin—pornography is okay, politics is not.'

I was still a Member of Parliament when Mrs Gandhi was assassinated on the morning of 31 October 1984. Despite my differences with her I was deeply distressed to hear of her dastardly murder at the hands of her own security guards, both Sikhs. If circumstances had allowed, I would most certainly have gone to condole with the family and pay my last tribute to her when her body was cremated. I had no great admiration for her as prime minister and am convinced that all that has gone wrong with the country emanated from her. She could be petty and vindictive, as she showed herself to be in her dealings with her widowed daughter-in-law, Maneka. She could be very discourteous to senior officials like Kewal Singh (retired ambassador to the United States), and Jagat Mehta (retired foreign secretary, whom she suspected of having let her down). She particularly enjoyed snubbing people who assumed she was their friend. She was nasty to Dom Moraes after he had written her biography; she accused Akbar Ahmed (Dumpy), a regular visitor to her house, of plotting her murder and issued orders that he was not to be allowed in. There were several occasions when I could have met her, as on the release of Sanjay Gandhi's biography by his wife Maneka, which I had helped edit. She expected me to be present on the occasion. I sensed she would be rude to me. I did not attend the function. She did not spare Maneka. It was the same at the release of the translation of her autobiography from French to English, to which I had written a preface. Mrs Gandhi had agreed with the publishers, Vision Books, to release it in her home. She expected me to be there. Again I sensed she was waiting for an opportunity to be nasty to me. I did not go for the release. She had to vent her spleen on the publisher. She told him before the assembled crowd that she would have nothing whatsoever to do with the book. It bore her name on the jacket.

When she died, I was unable to pay homage to Indira Gandhi in person because anti-Sikh violence, instigated by local leaders of her party, broke out all over the city. They spread false stories of Sikhs celebrating Mrs Gandhi's murder and distributing sweets and lighting up their houses; of Sikhs having poisoned Delhi's water supply, and of trainloads of Hindu corpses massacred by Sikhs coming to Delhi. Gangs of hired hoodlums were armed with iron rods and cans of gasoline to burn down gurdwaras, Sikh homes, shops and taxis, and to burn Sikhs alive. I was a marked man. The next morning I was warned that a mob was on its way to get me. In the nick of time Rolf Gauffin of the Swedish Embassy, whom I had never met before but who was a close friend of Romesh Thapar, came in his embassy car and took my wife and me away to his home in the embassy compound. I watched Mrs Gandhi's funeral on TV. I am pretty certain that, had she been alive, she would have gone round the city like her father, and stopped the carnage of thousands of innocent people. Her son, Rajiv Gandhi, stayed by his mother's body receiving VIPs. If he was not the author of the order to 'teach the Sikhs a lesson', he did nothing to countermand it.

It is no exaggeration to say that Indira's moods have often made and unmade the careers of people about her. Shibli wrote about this kind of awesome power to mould the destinies of the state in his lines to Noor Jehan, wife of Emperor Jehangir:

Us ki peyshani-i-nazuk peh jo parhti thi girah
Ja ke ban jati thi avraq-i-hakoomat peh shikan

When, in displeasure, wrinkles appeared on her forehead,
They were translated into commandments in documents of state.

RAJIV GANDHI
(1944–1991)

In the next few days, Rajiv Gandhi is likely to announce his decision to quit flying and enter politics. He had no interest in politics and had a very poor opinion of politicians. He was most reluctant to change his profession, and his wife, Sonia, was totally opposed to his going into the hurly burly of political life. However, he has at last decided to yield to the pressure put by members of the Congress Party. Mrs Gandhi's critics, particularly among the so-called intellectuals, have mounted a propaganda campaign questioning Rajiv Gandhi's entry into politics. 'He is only being brought in because he is the Prime Minister's son and Sanjay's brother,' they say. That may be so. But they overlook the fact that it is also his right as a citizen of India to do so. He is not—as the Opposition maintains—'succeeding' either his mother or his brother, but only offering himself (albeit reluctantly) to help as anyone else might in the organization. It would be a gross travesty of democratic principles to deny him rights enjoyed by all others simply because of his ancestry or relationship. He has yet to prove himself. And it will be for the people (not only his critics) to accept or reject him.

It is worth recalling that when Pandit Nehru first became president of the Indian National Congress, there was similar criticism that he had been chosen because he was Motilal's son. When Indira Gandhi succeeded Lal Bahadur Shastri, fairly and squarely beating Morarji Desai, it was said that she became prime minister because she was Jawaharlal's daughter.

And when Sanjay burst on the Indian political scene and established his unquestioned power over the party machine, similar insinuations were made against him.

But it was clear as daylight for anyone who wished to see that Nehru, Indira and Sanjay, each in his or her turn, were not imposed on the people but chosen by them. What could have been more democratic?

And now it will be Rajiv. There is little doubt that his way to the political path was paved by Sanjay Gandhi. People who believed in what Sanjay stood for hope that he will carry on the task that this valiant son of India left unfulfilled. Sanjay was much more than a Member of Parliament, the Prime Minister's right-hand man and leader of the Youth Congress. He had succeeded in firing the imagination of the people that they could, within their lifetime, convert the dream of a more prosperous and powerful India into a reality.

If the people are now eager to pass on the torch that Sanjay lit into the hands of his elder brother, they do so in the hope that Sanjay's unfinished mission will now be accomplished.

STILL THE BEST BET, IF HE LEARNS

The most significant thing that happened in the first month of 1987 was that people began to look for blemishes on Rajiv's face. This very month two years ago the same people were loud in praise of the many qualities he possessed—his good looks, his candour and courtesy—and assuring us that we were fortunate in having so forward-looking a man as him at the helm of our affairs. Why did the magic mirror, which once reflected his image as among the fairest of the fair, start showing warts and pimples?

Rajiv's own contribution to this change has been most noteworthy. Perhaps his massive victory at the polls gave him an illusion of invulnerability. He succumbed to the temptation of riding roughshod over dissenters, ignored institutions and traditions of governance, appointed friends unknown to the public to important public positions, and unceremoniously fired those whose vibes did not please him. He began to pronounce with authority on subjects with which he had little familiarity. The subjantawala destroyed the image of a modest young man eager to learn. Said a south Indian friend to me: 'A man who till the other day only knew how to handle the joystick in a cockpit can hardly be expected to deliver learned sermons from the world's pulpits.'

Rajiv's image has by no means suffered irreparable damage. He should know that he still remains our best bet to lead the country. He can afford to dismiss the rantings of politicians but he must take the near-unanimous criticism by the press, the trahison des clercs—the revolt of civil servants—more seriously.

The press enjoys more credibility with the people than politicians. Civil servants have taken a lot of mauling from politicians and will not take any more. I raise my glass to toast the Venkateswarans of India: 'God give us men!
Men whom the lust of office does not kill.'

V. P. SINGH
(1931–2008)

My first encounter with V. P. Singh was some time in the spring of 1985. He was minister of finance; I, a little-noticed backbencher in the Rajya Sabha. It was on a Thursday morning when the prime minister is present in the Upper House during question hour and attendance is higher than on other days. Down the list of questions was one regarding the non-clearance by Customs of woollen garments and blankets sent by Sikh communities in England and Iran for the victims of the anti-Sikh violence following Mrs Gandhi's assassination. Most of those parcels were addressed to me by name but despite frantic efforts to get them released, the People's Relief Committee had failed to get around the bureaucrats of the Delhi Administration to issue a certificate of clearance. Thousands of men, women and children had spent the winter months shivering in the cold while sweaters and rugs sent for them gathered dust in the Customs sheds. That morning I had received a notice from the Customs demanding ₹75,000 as demurrage for not having cleared goods sent to me. Understandably, I was in a highly agitated frame of mind.

The question had been put by me. It was answered by V. P. Singh's deputy, Janardhan Poojary, in the usually devious way ministers adopt to answer awkward questions. The parcels, he said, were not addressed to any person and no one had taken the responsibility for clearing them. I raised my hand to put in a supplementary. Fortunately for me, the gargantuan-sized Vishwajeet Singh of the Congress (I) roared at the top of his voice to say that the minister's statement was incorrect and that he knew that most of the crates were addressed to me. As I stood up and waved the Customs demand on me and letters showing the callousness of Delhi Administration babus, there were loud cries of 'shame' from all sides of the House. I saw V. P. Singh turn to Prime Minister Rajiv Gandhi and whisper something in his ear. He waved for Poojary to sit down and took the floor himself. He apologized to the House for the delay and promised that the entire consignment would be cleared within twenty-four hours. That evening he rang up and told me that if the consignment had not been cleared by next morning, I should let him know. The next morning, the secretary of the ministry and V. P. Singh again rang me up to find out whether their orders had been carried out. They were, with dispatch I had never known. By the afternoon, we had tons of sweaters and blankets in the godowns of the People's Relief Committee.

Although the winter was over, we were able to provide every single afflicted family with clothing for several winters to come.

That one encounter was good enough for me to form a most favourable impression of the man. Till then I had only known him through newspaper reports and had heard him speak in Parliament on matters of commerce and finance. He was among the most competent ministers, but by no means the most outstanding on the Treasury Benches. There were many others who came as well prepared as he, and quite a few with greater powers of oratory.

It was after the Fairfax affair and his sudden transfer from the Finance to the Defence Ministry followed by his ouster from the government, suspension, and dismissal from the Congress Party that, from being one of the many possible candidates for succession to Rajiv Gandhi, he emerged as the most likely successor.

This was not entirely through his own efforts. After Fairfax came Bofors, the German submarine deal, the Bachchan brothers' business morals: Rajiv's troubles came not in single spies but in the proverbial battalions.

He tried to ward them off, waving his arms like one attacked by a swarm of hornets. And was stung all over his face. The once Mr Clean acquired a visage swollen with innuendos of corruption, sheltering corrupt friends and insulting the president. Instead of relying on the advice of trustworthy tellers of unpleasant truths he lent ears to self-seekers like Dinesh Singh ever eager to return to the Treasury Benches—and the likes of loudmouthed K. K. Tiwari and the greasy Kalpnath Rai to bray to their trumpets. Within two years of his spectacular victory at the polls, Rajiv Gandhi achieved the incredible by turning from a vote-catcher to a vote-loser, from being the Congress

Party's best bet to remain in power to its biggest handicap. Those that began to desert his sinking ship were not rats but men who felt that the only chance of keeping it was to change the pilot.

It would appear that from the day V. P. Singh was inducted into the central Cabinet, he took his role as that of a broom to clean the Congress stables of corruption. In a short poem in Hindi published early in January 1985 entitled 'Jhaaran ka Dhan' (wealth of the duster), he wrote:

> Let me lie where I am
> It is only dust that I have gathered
> If you manhandle me
> Even this may go out of hand and be scattered

I spent some hours talking to one of V. P. Singh's closest friends since his schooldays and cross-checking facts and opinions with V. P. Singh's wife, Sita Kumari, and their family friends.

Vishwanath Pratap Singh was born at Allahabad on 25 June 1931. His father was the Raja of Daiya, a large zamindari yielding a revenue of about ₹2 lakh per year. He had two wives: one bore him two sons, C. S. P. Singh, who later became a judge of the Allahabad High Court (then the youngest judge of any high court in the country; he met a tragic end); and Vishwanath Pratap Singh. The second wife had three sons, Sant Bux, Harbux and Rajendra Singh. They were Gaharwar Thakurs, a branch of Rathore Rajputs descended from Manik Chand of Kannauj, brother of Raja Jai Chand. The siblings from the two wives of the Raja of Daiya lived under the same roof in absolute harmony. VP's hero and guide-philosopher of his earlier days was his stepbrother, Sant Bux, a Congress Party member of the Lok Sabha.

VP was torn away from under his father's roof when he was only five years old. The neighbouring Raja of Manda (about ₹3 lakh annual revenue) being issueless, adopted him as his son. He forbade VP from having anything to do with his real parents and brothers and, being tubercular himself, kept his adopted son at a distance. For a few months he was looked after by an English couple, Mr and Mrs Cook, and thereafter by Amar Singh Mathur, a civil servant who was appointed his guardian. He lived with the Mathurs and came to look upon them as his real parents. VP recounts an incident when he was a student at Allahabad High School. One day a boy in a senior class came to see him and introduced himself, 'Don't tell anyone, but I am your elder brother, Chandra Shekhar Prasad.' So strict had been the segregation that VP had been unable to recognize his real brother CSP. Thereafter, the two met regularly, but in secret. When the Raja Bahadur of Manda died in 1941, the adoption was challenged in court by collaterals. The estate had, in any event, been so badly mismanaged that it had fallen into debt and was placed under government control through the court of wards.

It was now the turn of the Raja of Daiya to play the heavy-handed father. He manipulated Amar Singh Mathur's recall to service to claim custody of his son.

VP, then only ten, fought back. He clung to his chair and refused to leave the Mathur household. He had to be forcibly lifted and taken to Daiya. It was ten years later when the Mathurs, then settled in Delhi, invited him to their daughter's wedding that he was able to resume communication with the family that had been closest to him. The scars these traumatic childhood experiences left on VP's mind remained unhealed for many years.

Even back among his family, VP had to be constantly guarded by gunmen because of threats to his life by rival claimants to the gaddi of Manda. During these years of his childhood and adolescence he lived apart from other boys under the watchful eye of a guardian-cum-tutor. The little outdoor life he had was with his brothers whom he visited periodically and, like others of the landed gentry, when he went for an occasional shoot. Having bagged his quota of a tiger, a few panthers and other game which was noblesse oblige for his class, he sickened of blood sport and gave it up.

After the death of his adoptive father, VN (the initials by which he was known before the press changed them to VP) was sent to Colonel Brown's School in Dehra Dun. It was a prestigious preparatory school from which boys went onto the Royal Indian Military Academy, the Doon or other upper-class schools. After some years at Colonel Brown's, he shifted to the Boys' High School, Allahabad, and then to Uday Pratap College in Varanasi. The institution had been set up by the

Raja of Bhinga for the education of Thakur Rajputs with the specific condition that the principal would always be an Englishman. When VP moved from Dehra Dun to Varanasi, his Hindi was somewhat halting. That was taken care of by his tutor-guardian, Pandit Vijay Shankar Mishra. He was also somewhat weak in mathematics and took special coaching from Rajwant Singh, whose son, being a classmate, became a lifelong friend. VP was a slogger and always managed to be in the top half of his class. He was a good debater and always walked away with first prizes both in Hindi and English.

VP stood out in school as a quiet loner who took life more seriously than schoolboys of his age. He was a shy, fair boy with curly hair, always dressed in a spotless white shirt and shorts. The boys referred to him as Ajoriya ka bachcha—child of moonlight. Though an adolescent, he was serious-minded and did well enough to get merits in most subjects. While still himself a student, he opened a school in his native Daiya and spent his vacations teaching village schoolchildren. He forbade students from addressing him as 'Raja Saab' or 'Hakim' and preferred being known simply as 'Masterji'. He and his brother Sant Bux also began to address meetings in favour of the abolition of zamindari, which upset many zamindars. After doing his matriculation in 1946 and securing a first class and distinction in mathematics, he joined college from where two years later he took his intermediate examination in arts subjects, securing a position in the merit list of UP and distinction in mathematics. He went on to Allahabad University, from where he graduated in 1950 and got his LLB. Throughout his academic life he was under the surveillance of his bodyguards and lived in 'Aish Mahal', Allahabad, residence of the Manda Raja. He was driven to college in a state Chevrolet or a phaeton; his guards waited for him outside his school classrooms and drove back with him. Loneliness forced him to cultivate hobbies like photography and painting. He also took guitar lessons from Mazumdar, a staff artist of All India Radio.

Though qualified as a lawyer, VP never practised law. 'He was temperamentally unsuited to making money out of other people's troubles,' says his friend.

V. P. Singh's father arranged a marriage for him, with Sita Kumari, daughter of the Raja of Peogarh-Madaria in Rajasthan. Those that jibe at V. P. Singh ancestry being a descendant of Raja Jai Chand should know that Sita Kumari is a Sisodia Rajput descended from Rana Pratap of Udaipur. Sita had studied up to higher secondary at Sofia College, Ajmer. Though both were educated, neither groom nor bride was consulted nor had a glimpse of each other till after the nuptials on 25 June 1955. Sita Kumari was then eighteen, V. P. Singh twenty-four.

Sita Kumari is a remarkably vivacious and attractive lady in her early fifties and far too outspoken for a wife of a politician. 'Family life?' she exclaimed in answer to my question. 'Very little of that. When I married him he was already neck deep in social work and politics. From dawn to dusk he was receiving visitors or attending meetings. We hardly ever ate together. His meals were left on the dining table for him to eat whenever he had the time.' VP and Sita Kumari have two sons, Ajay Singh (b. 1957), a chartered accountant now living in New York, and Abhai Singh (b. 1958), currently a doctor in the All India Institute of Medical Sciences (AIIMS) of New Delhi.

Sita Kumari talks nostalgically of the months the family spent in Poona with a family friend. 'The two families lived in two rooms. My husband attended Physics classes at the Fergusson College—he was always keen on science subjects (he got a first class in BSc)—we women ran the house, looked after the children and went out together to the pictures in the evenings.'

'Surely, with your princely backgrounds, you must have had a horde of servants to do the household chores!' I said.

'Believe me, from the day I married VP I have done all the buying of vegetables and stores and cooked every meal myself. He gave away all his land in Bhoodan. There has never been anything princely in our style of living.'

There is certainly nothing aristocratic or upper class about the ministerial bungalow No.1 at Teen Murti Marg which has been V. P. Singh's home for the last two years. Cane chairs on the veranda with only a stuffed turtle on the ground. A perky little snow-white Pomeranian named Fifi who barks a welcome at every visitor and then insists he pet her all the time. The sitting room is as the Central Public Works Department furnished it with the bare minimum of sofas, chairs, and a large table. Dominating the room is a colour-print of Indira Gandhi. On the side-walls a couple of oil paintings made by V. P. Singh (one of a girl's head only showing her thick black hair). A few gewgaws on the side tables of no artistic or material value. Sita Kumari brings in the tea tray herself and discreetly retires to another room to let visitors talk to her husband. She re-enters as people are about to take their leave.

I remarked on her lack of jewellery: she wears no rings, necklaces, bracelets or earrings—only a mangalsutra. 'You must have been given a lot of jewellery on your marriage. What have you done with it?'

Her eyes sparkled and she laughed as if she were telling me of a great windfall in her fortunes. 'Yes, I had some jewellery when I came as a bride. I hardly ever wore it. I was taking it in a box to wear at a wedding. The box was stolen at night at the railway station. I lost everything.'

'You seem remarkably cheerful about it.'

'What to do? What's gone is gone. Why cry over it? I don't miss it one bit.'

She told me of his daily routine. 'He gets up around seven and reads the English and Hindi papers. Prayers? No, no prayers. Some exercise. He used to do weight-lifting; now it is only a few yoga asanas. Then it is just people and more people. Meetings and more meetings. He never sees TV or listens to the radio.'

I asked her if she knew of any books that had influenced her husband's outlook. She paused for a while before replying. 'He reads books on psychology. But the only book he has read over and over again is *How to be Happy Though Human*.'

'He couldn't have had many friends.'

'He knows a lot of people but has very few close friends,' she replied. 'Ranmat Singh has always been very close. Then there was Asif Ansari who became a judge of the Allahabad High Court. He died in 1978.'

'Who were the men who influenced him most?' 'Most of all it was his own elder brother, Sant Bux Singh. Then there were Jayaprakash Narayan and Vinoba Bhave. Lal Bahadur Shastri was his political guide and philosopher when he first entered political life.'

VP's initiation into politics came indirectly through Lal Bahadur Shastri in whose parliamentary constituency Manda and Daiya lay—and directly through his elder brother Sant Bux who resigned his job with Lever Brothers to seek a political future. They did not share a common political commitment. Sant Bux inclined towards socialism; VP preferred to toe the Congress Party line. He attracted Shastri's attention when he gave his estate to Bhoodan—and when Vinoba Bhave refused to take all of it, gave what had been returned to him to the school he had set up.

'Don't say I and them,' Vinoba told him. 'Say we.'

He also gave away part of the Manda Palace for the Lal Bahadur Shastri Seva Niketan. He got seven and a half lakh rupees in compensation for the zamindari taken over by the government and thought he would try his hand at real estate business. He did a certain amount of buying and selling of land in New Delhi till Sant Bux decided to fight the 1967 parliamentary elections from Fatehpur. This was VP's first experience of elections. Sant Bux won an easy victory. Two years later, VP himself stood on a Congress ticket for the UP Vidhan Sabha and found himself an MLA. And two years later (1971) both brothers fought the Lok Sabha elections and won. VP's constituency was Phulpur (Allahabad). VP took his parliamentary responsibilities seriously and tried to specialize in science, technology and energy. In 1974 when Mrs Gandhi was looking for a UP Thakur to counterbalance Dinesh Singh's hold on the community, she consulted Kamalapati Tripathi and Dev Kanta Barua, then president of the Congress. Kamalapati recommended Sant Bux. Barua, without any prompting, suggested V. P. Singh. She accepted Barua's recommendation and much to everyone's, including VP's, surprise appointed him Deputy Minister of Commerce. She knew if she appointed Sant Bux, VP would have been very happy. If she appointed VP, his elder brother was bound to feel peeved. She enjoyed creating discord.

VP remained minister throughout the Emergency: his only unpleasant experience was having his pocket picked in Lucknow and having to borrow money from a friend. He paid the price for his support of the Emergency and, like Mrs Gandhi, was swept out of Parliament by the Janata wave. He continued to fight the Janata regime and was thrice arrested and interred in Naini Jail. When Mrs Gandhi swept back to power, VP regained the Allahabad seat. It was at Mrs Gandhi's insistence that he gave up his seat in Parliament and took over as chief minister of Uttar Pradesh and was elected member of the state Vidhan Sabha. He resigned the chief ministership in June 1982 as a sequel to two massacres in one night, one of them of a Harijan family. At the time there were few politicians who would do that sort of thing.

Seven months later he was made Minister of Commerce and later returned to the Rajya Sabha. He was president of the UP Congress Committee when Mrs Gandhi was assassinated. He was the real architect of the Congress Party's victory in the elections that followed in December 1984. Eighty-three of UP's eighty-five seats in Parliament, including Rajiv Gandhi's from Amethi, were won by the Congress. He was Rajiv Gandhi's choice as finance minister in place of Pranab Mukherjee, who had forfeited his trust. It was to his credit that the first budget he presented, though totally at variance with Pranab's way of thinking, was warmly supported and welcomed by the captains of industry.

Nani Palkhivala, a director of Tatas and the country's best-known expert of budgetary finance, who always manages to pick holes in most budgets, was full of praise for VP's first budget.

VP's troubles began with his determination to go for tax evaders and violators of foreign exchange rules. His victims included the aged and highly respected industrialist S. L. Kirloskar, and L. M. Thapar, who was uncomfortably close to the prime minister. The net began to tighten around more people in the prime minister's inner circle, notably the Bachchan brothers.

There can be little doubt that VP's shift to the Defence Ministry and his subsequent sacking was to prevent further exposures of skeletons in Rajiv's cupboard.

Another short verse from his own pen summarizes his plight:

I have been cut into pieces
But my value remains the same;
I was a solid coin
Now I have become small change.

The truth about financial skulduggery remains unknown. It cannot be controverted that V. P. Singh has emerged from the imbroglio as a man with a clean image and Rajiv Gandhi as one not-so-clean as he was believed to be when he first took office. In four lines VP sums up corruption among the rich:

> Who does not convert
> 'Black' into 'White'?
> Some do it by cooking their accounts,
> Others by the help of a hair dye.

Has V. P. Singh a political philosophy? Is he left or right of centre? Or a middle-headed opportunist unconcerned with the means he adopts and the allies he chooses to pedestal himself to prime ministership? Journalists like M. J. Akbar have accused him of consorting with right-wing anti-Muslim parties like the BJP and the RSS. Kamalapati Tripathi, himself the most devious of politicians, has charged him with knowing no more than the first three letters of the English alphabet: A for Amitabh, B for Bofors, C for Chaddha. Going by reports of his speeches appearing in the press, one may be forgiven if one agrees with Tripathi's assessment. 'What am I to do?' asks VP, 'if all that pressmen everywhere pick out of my speeches are Amitabh-Ajitabh, Bofors and Chaddhas because they think they are in the news and whatever else I have to say about the state of the nation is not. I have very clear notions of my priorities.'

I asked VP to spell out his socio-political plan of action. Uppermost in his mind is changing the system that breeds the anti-people nexus of politicians and big business. The big business and politician combine vitiates not only the polity but also the economy. VP's remedy for this is state funding of politics, and extension of democratic processes to all levels. Political parties like the Congress have had no elections for many years. As a result, power has remained concentrated in a few hands. Instead of recognizing efficiency as the criterion to entrust power to such people, the system extends patronage only to those it can count on for support.

A party should sustain itself by what its members contribute. Or the state should fund them during elections in proportion to their prior performances. Their accounts must be fully and regularly audited and it must be ensured that a clique does not consolidate its hold on it. The chief executive of every party should be elected periodically; otherwise the party will become feudal in character and unable to serve the people. The democratic process should be taken down to the grassroots. For seventeen years UP has had no zila parishad election; thousands of municipalities have likewise continued to malfunction because their members have not renewed their mandate. Such lethargy deadens democratic reflexes. We should amend our Constitution to ensure elections at all levels down to the village panchayats. Entrusting full powers to elected bodies will inevitably bring the administration closer to the people. 'Issues must go beyond milestones of elections,' says V. P. Singh.

He is equally concerned with the surfacing of religious and caste considerations in the selection of candidates and their patterns of voting. He thinks that we should give serious consideration to proportional representation as a possible solution.

Industry should likewise be democratized with fuller representation to workers on boards of directors, and they should be ensured a fair share of the fruits of their toil. This will effectively curb irresponsible trade unionism.

The agricultural sector and prices of agricultural produce need a thorough overhaul. When fixing prices of produce, it is not good enough to only add up prices of inputs. The cost of living, comprising items of men's consumption like the price of cloth, should also be taken into account. Special care has to be taken of unorganized landless labour, and Scheduled Castes and Tribes. They must be given possession of land they till and their 18 per cent quota of seats should remain available to them at all times and not be filled by others.

Communalism? We have communalized politics and politicians rouse communal passions to retain power. If instead of being organized on religious lines we were to reorganize our society on the basis of common economic interests—farmers, weavers, factory workers, etc.— we would with one stroke kill the canker of communalism and bring the fruits of development to the people.

VP scoffs at insinuations against his secularism. 'In my home

Muslims were as acceptable as Hindus. During Muharram tazias used to pass in front of our home and I with my father would go to pay respects. In Manda the estate had its own tazia also. When violence broke out in Moradabad, I offered to resign my chief ministership.'

After a pause he added with deliberation, 'Anyone who harbours communal prejudices has no right to call himself civilized.'

I asked him about the kind of reception he has had during his tour of different states: Bihar, UP, Bengal, MP, Karnataka, Gujarat and Rajasthan. He did not exaggerate. 'It is difficult to assess crowds. What is more important than the numbers who turn up to hear me is that all over the country they want a drastic change in their governance.'

I asked him of his reaction to his critics in the press. He brushed the question aside: 'They say whatever comes to their mind; I cannot answer all of them. I talk to the people and they give me the answers.'

GIANI ZAIL SINGH
(1916–1994)

When Giani Zail Singh was sworn in as the seventh rashtrapati of India on 25 July 1980, I was rash enough to forecast that despite his modest education and inability to speak English, he would prove to be the most popular president the country had had thus far—outstripping the suave Rajendra Prasad, the scholarly S. Radhakrishnan and Zakir Hussain, garrulous V. V. Giri and Neelam Sanjiva Reddy and the all-too pliable Fakhruddin Ali Ahmad. He started off with a bang. On Thursday, 8 July 1980, he came to the Central Hall of Parliament to bid farewell to fellow parliamentarians and announce the termination of his long association with the Congress Party. He was a few minutes late and was visibly embarrassed as Prime Minister Indira Gandhi was addressing the assemblage.

She further embarrassed him by her words of welcome: 'See, he is blushing like a bride!' So the Giani did, to the roots of his glossy black dyed beard. His farewell speech to fellow politicians was a tour de force of sentimental oratory the like of which is rarely heard these days. He ended with a reference to Mrs Gandhi's quip about his blushing, admitting that he felt like an Indian bride taking leave of her parents, brothers and sisters when every member of the family is in tears. 'You have decided to retire me from politics; however, mine will be a kind of a shaahee retirement,' he concluded.

His first few months as rashtrapati were roses, roses all the way. Wherever he went, he was welcomed by mammoth crowds. He regaled them with rustic anecdotes, Urdu couplets, Persian and Punjabi poetry, quotations from sacred Sanskrit texts, the Quran and the Granth Sahib. Here at last was a 'people's rashtrapati', earthy, one who could talk on the same level to the peasant and the artisan; enter into a dialogue with the pandit, the maulvi and the granthi. The only class with which he neither tried nor was capable of making an equation was the westernized woggery.

They cracked their Sardarji jokes at his expense at their cocktail parties. He often exposed himself to their jibes as he did when criticizing the Darwinian theory of our descent from the apes: 'How could the Buddha be a progeny of a monkey?' he asked naively.

But few wags dared to take him on in public because they knew they could not hope to match him in witty repartee. He ignored their existence.

The one thing that had irked the sophisticated sections of society was his exaggerated deference to the 'royal family'. He said he would be willing to sweep the floor if Mrs Gandhi so desired and acknowledged the then seeming heir-apparent, Sanjay, as his rehnuma (guide). Few people realized that darbardari (flattery) was deeply ingrained in his psyche as he was born and brought up in the courtly atmosphere of Faridkot Raj where only sycophancy and cunning ensured survival.

Within a few months, things began to go awry. It was his own community which had earlier lauded his elevation as the first Sikh rashtrapati that began to deride him. The Akalis launched their 'dharma yuddha morcha' against the government. The Giani mocked them: 'Akali, akal ke khalee (Akalis are empty headed)'. They retaliated by describing him as a sarkari Sikh and the prime minister's rubber stamp. Akali demonstrations against the ninth Asiad gave Bhajan Lal's Haryana constabulary freedom to harass all Sikhs coming to Delhi by rail and road. For the first time in the history of independent India, Sikhs came to be discriminated against. It was ironic that this should have started when a Sikh presided over the country. His stock among the Sikh community began to decline. Then events overtook him with rapid succession—Operation Bluestar was followed by Operation Woodrose to comb the Punjab countryside for terrorists.

Gianiji had been kept in the dark about Bluestar but the Sikhs held him responsible for it. High priests of the Takhts summoned him to explain why he should not be declared a tankhaiya. In many gurdwaras posters with his pictures were laid out on the floor at the entrance for worshippers to tread on. His TV appearance visiting the Harmandir Sahib after the carnage wearing a rose in his sherwani caused a wave of resentment. He was virtually written off by his community. Then came the assassination of Mrs Indira Gandhi followed by the massacre of Sikhs in towns and cities of northern India. Being a Sikh, the Giani had to suffer the odium with which Hindus began to regard his community.

Hardly had the country returned to normalcy and the Giani regained his equipoise, than the new prime minister, Rajiv Gandhi, began to exhibit boorishness unbecoming of a young man of his lineage towards an elder to whom he initially owed his position. The Giani felt isolated and unwanted. I was pretty certain that he was looking for a suitable opportunity to resign and to go out of the Rashtrapati Bhavan with the same fanfare with which he had entered it. I was wrong. He stepped out of his mansion not with the proverbial bang, but not with a whimper either.

In the last six months, he gave Rajiv Gandhi and his advisers a taste of their own medicine and many sleepless nights. What is more, if they had any illusions of making up for lost sleep after Gianiji quit Rashtrapati Bhavan, they were in for a nasty surprise. Unlike his predecessors, who disappeared into pastoral oblivion after their retirement, Gianiji was a retired president living in the capital and determined to level his score with the Prime Minister. I foresaw Gianiji becoming the patron saint of those disenchanted with the regime.

Although he did not fulfil my prophecy of being the most popular president of the republic, he will undoubtedly go down in the pages of history as the most talked about president of the Indian republic. What was there in this man of humble origins and little academic learning that helped him overcome one obstacle after another and pedestal himself to triumph, to reach the pinnacle of aspiration and become the head of state? I will let incidents in his life speak for him.

Zail Singh was an active worker of Praja Mandal of the erstwhile Faridkot state. The raja had personally ordered him to be jailed. When India became independent and Faridkot was merged into the Patiala and East Punjab States Union (PEPSU), the central government was looking for suitable men to run the new state. Sardar Vallabhbhai Patel summoned Zail Singh. Zail Singh did not have the money to buy a third-class return ticket from Faridkot to Delhi and had to ask friends for a loan. In Delhi, he stayed in Gurdwara Sis Ganj. He did not have money to hire a tonga to take him to Sardar Patel's residence at five in the morning. He walked the entire four miles and was late for his appointment. Sardar Patel's daughter brusquely dismissed him. It was the kindly secretary, V. Shankar, who let him see the deputy prime minister. Zail Singh was told that he was being made minister of state in PEPSU. He walked back to the railway station to return to Faridkot. He never looked back. He did not forget his humble origins nor let power go to his head.

Success was to him a gift given by the Great Guru, not something owed to him by virtue of his abilities.

One of his favourite couplets warns one of the dangers of hubris:

Jin mein ho jaata hai andaz-e-khudaee paida
Hum ne dekha hai voh butt toot jaate hain.

Mortals who allow notions of divinity to germinate in them
We have seen those idols shattered and come to grief.

There is not even a suspicion of arrogance or self-esteem in this man. Besides humility, his faith in religion taught him to be honest and truthful. He is one of the breed of politicians, now almost extinct, who though handling vast sums of money never feathered his own nest nor those of his relatives. He owns no house, flat or tract of land except the little he inherited.

Nobody has ever accused him of telling a lie. As a junior minister, Zail Singh set about assiduously cultivating the support of the lower and discriminated castes. He is a Ramgarhia (carpenter). Punjab has always been dominated by Jat and Sikh politics constipated with caste considerations. Zail Singh broke the Jat hegemony over the state and successfully mocked Akali pretensions of being thekedars (monopolists) of the Khalsa Panth. He was able to convince the Sikhs that he was a better Sikh than all the Akali leaders put together. His speeches were always full of quotations from the *Gurbani* and episodes from Sikh history. No other politician, either from the Akali party or the Congress, could build this kind of Gursikh image for himself as did the Giani. By the time he made his presence felt in the state, a precedent had been established that the chief minister of Punjab should be a Sikh. There was no better Sikh than Giani Zail Singh to fill the role.

Zail Singh's six-year tenure as the chief minister was perhaps the most peaceful and prosperous the state has ever seen. They were the years of the Green Revolution. They were also the years without morchas, bandhs or strikes. The Giani was able to rekindle pride in Punjabiyat. From England he acquired the mortal remains of Madan Lal Dhingra who had been hanged for the murder of Curzon Wyllie, and of Udham Singh, hanged for the murder of Sir Michael O'Dwyer, governor of Punjab at the time of Jallianwala Bagh, and he raised martyrs' memorials over them. He sought out the long-forgotten and ailing mother of Bhagat Singh, gave her a handsome grant and had her honoured as Punjab Mata—Mother of Punjab. The road connecting Anandpur to Fatehgarh was named Guru Gobind Singh Marg; horses believed to be descendants of the Guru's steed were taken along the marg for the populace to see and marvel at.

A new township, Baba Ajit Singh Nagar, was named after the Guru's eldest son. Massive keertan darbars were organized all over the state. In his eagerness to wrest the Akali monopoly over the affairs of the Khalsa Panth, he unwittingly set in motion a Sikh revivalism which turned into fundamentalism under Jarnail Singh Bhindranwale.

Gianiji could not have foreseen this development, much less wished it, because his relations with Punjabi Hindus including the somewhat anti-Sikh Mahasha press of Jalandhar, remained extremely cordial. And if gossip is to be believed, more than cordial with the smaller Muslim community. Giani Zail Singh achieved the incredible: he had no enemies. Besides being the Punjabi paradigm of a dostaan da dost (of friends the friendliest) he had the knack of winning over detractors. Even in the heyday of his power as chief minister and home minister, he never tried to settle scores with people who had persecuted or humiliated him. He won them over by granting them favours and making them ashamed of themselves. If there was anything he could do for anyone, he never hesitated to do it. He had an incredibly good memory for names and faces. He was able to gain friends by simply recognizing people he had met briefly.

During the Emergency, while he had put many people in jail, he went to see them. He sent a wedding gift to P. S. Badal's daughter when her father was in prison and went to receive the baraat at the house of a friend's daughter in Kalka when her father was locked up. If he heard a friend was sick he would find time to visit him in hospital and quietly slip a bundle of currency notes under his pillow. Virtually the only man he was unable to win over was Darbara Singh who succeeded him as chief minister of Punjab.

To describe Gianiji as a far-sighted statesman would be an exaggeration; to describe him as a cunning politician would be grossly unfair because the stock-in-trade of a cunning politician is the ability to tell a blatant lie. And the one thing no one can accuse Gianiji of is falsehood. He is best described as a shrewd judge of men and events.

After Mrs Gandhi's murder, there were many claimants to the prime ministership. Oddly enough, one of the seniormost civil servants at the time and later a confidant of the present prime minister even suggested to Gianiji that he take over the prime ministership himself. Sensing the anti-Sikh climate of the day, it was Gianiji who brushed aside this inane suggestion and decided to offer it to Rajiv Gandhi in the belief that as the descendant of Nehru and Indira Gandhi, he would be best suited to hold the country together.

And when the Opposition tried to put him up for a second term and Congress dissidents assured him of a substantial vote from the Congress Party, he carefully weighed his prospects before turning it down. He was not a gambler; he played to win. It was the same when pressure was brought on him to dismiss the prime minister or permit his prosecution on charges of corruption. Gianiji had little to lose and he could have made things very hot for Rajiv Gandhi. He refused to succumb to temptation, teaching Rajiv a lesson for his bad behaviour, because he felt that the nation's future was paramount and India was more important than Rajiv Gandhi or Zail Singh.

He has often quoted a couplet to the effect that while he put a rose in the palms of Rajiv Gandhi, Rajiv took a stone to hurt him. There is an equally apt couplet for him to mull over in his days of retirement:

Zakhmee hue jo hont to mahsoos yeh hua
Chooma tha maine phool ko deevanagi ke sath.

It was the bruises on my lips that made me comprehend
With what thoughtlessness I had kissed the rose.

DR A. P. J. ABDUL KALAM
(1931–2015)

Having seen and heard him on TV and read his short book, one cannot but conclude that the next president of India is not going to be like any one of his predecessors. Nor indeed like the president of any other country, least of all that of the largest democracy in the world. He is not impressive to look at; with his tousled, untidy hair and buck teeth he looks more like a character from a comic strip than the head of state. Though his speeches do not rise to heights of oratory, they do manage—like Mahatma Gandhi's mumblings—to get to the hearts of the common people. His own achievements inspire respect and hope: if the son of a poor boatman from Rameswaram can make it to the palatial residence of the president atop Raisina Hill, why not I? That, in short, is the message that comes through *Ignited Minds*.

Did Abdul Kalam have a role model? When asked by a child who his favourite character in the Mahabharata was, Kalam replied without hesitation: Vidura. It may be recalled that Vidura was the son of a low-caste handmaiden. Kalam was impressed by him because he 'showed grit against the wrongdoings of authority and had the courage to differ when everyone else chose to surrender before the tyranny of adharma'. He was also the wisest of the brothers. Kalam must be fully aware that he belongs to a discriminated-against minority and owes his selection as a candidate for the presidency of our republic largely to the covering up of the sins of adharma committed by the members of the ruling coalition in Gujarat. He will have plenty of opportunities to bring people who pursue the path of evil in the name of dharma back on the right track in a secular democracy.

Kalam is a dreamer of great dreams, not for himself but his country. Unlike most of his countrymen who boast of their achievements, he is refreshingly free of vainglory. He plays down all he has done by way of scientific research in missile and nuclear technology. He gives credit to the team he has worked with and pays homage to Indians who have achieved spectacular success in mathematics, medicine and other sciences. All of them were dreamers who, against great odds, translated their dreams into reality. He exhorts the young of India to be inspired by their example. No matter how wild and impractical your dreams may appear at first sight, persist in giving them practical shape. If you think the waters of the oceanic Brahmaputra should be brought to green the arid and sandy wastes of Rajasthan or slake the thirst of Tamilians, get down to laying canals across the length and breadth of India. Nothing ventured, nothing gained is his motto.

He suggests a list of his priorities: increase agricultural production to keep ahead of the increasing population, make electric power available in every village, provide education and healthcare to everyone (it will automatically bring down the rate of increase in population), take information of the latest technologies down to the masses and make the country powerful in nuclear, space and defence technologies. He is convinced that this can be achieved in the next eighteen years, by 2020, if we have the will and determination to do so.

Kalam is not blind to our failures. He lists them with equal candour: 'Lament, my friend, at the passing away of a generation of politicians with a voice, vision and reach that went far beyond our borders. Lament at our state-sponsored, abnormal and paranoid fixation with a particular country that has blinded us to the rest of the world, including the third world, which we used to head not so long ago. And weep softly at what we have reduced ourselves to in the comity of nations. For a large country with a billion people, a country with a thriving industry and a large pool of scientific talent, a country, moreover, that is a nuclear power, India does not count for as much as it should. In terms of our influence in world affairs, probably no other country is so far below its potential as we are.'

Kalam, however, is convinced that 'purity' is possible even in politics. 'I believe if the nation forms a second vision today,' he writes, 'leaders of a stature to suit our ambition will appear once again, in all walks of life, including politics.'

Ignited Minds will fire the minds of the young to whom it is primarily addressed. However, one hopes that like Atal Behari Vajpayee who mercifully stopped writing poetry after he became prime minister, Kalam too will stop his little attempts at versification after he takes over as President of India.

JAYAPRAKASH NARAYAN
(1902–1979)

Most of the leaders who today heap words of praise on Jayaprakash had few kind words to say about him till he became a force to be reckoned with. They called him confused, muddle-headed, indecisive, inconsequential, reactionary. Whatever he may be, he is also the conscience-keeper of the nation.

Rumours of a young firebrand blowing up bridges and looting arsenals began floating around soon after the arrests of Mahatma Gandhi and other Congress leaders in the Quit India Movement in 1942. This was wartime and there was strict censorship of the papers. Even 'loose talk' could land a person in jail. Nevertheless, vastly exaggerated stories of terrorist activities in the eastern provinces continued to circulate in the Punjab, at the time ruled by the Unionist government proud of its loyalty to the British. Besides the loyalists, there were others who disapproved of the Quit India Movement and believed that India should first help the Allied Powers defeat the fascists and then force the British out of India. I subscribed to this school of thought and much as I admired people with the guts to do or die, I disapproved of what they were doing. Consequently, my emotional admiration for Jayaprakash Narayan was qualified by rational disapproval of his acts. My reaction to the news of his arrest was very muddled.

It was a bit of a shock to learn that Jayaprakash was in Lahore where I was then living. The massive walls of the Lahore Fort separated him from his countrymen. We discovered this when H. R. Pardivala, a socialist lawyer from Bombay, was arrested and brought to Lahore. His only crime was to have moved a petition of habeas corpus for the release of Jayaprakash Narayan. It was Pardivala who told us that Jayaprakash was being put through the third degree by the Punjab police. He had been beaten, kept awake for several days and nights, and made to sit naked on blocks of ice. He had withstood it all and refused to divulge anything against his fellow conspirators. All at once, whatever reservations I had about his politics, my admiration for his manly qualities swept them aside.

Another twelve years were to elapse before I got the chance to meet him. By then my admiration for him bordered on worship. Here was a man who had disagreed with Gandhi, spurned the chance of becoming deputy prime minister in Nehru's Cabinet and had instead chosen the vagrant path of socialism. He had the courage to renounce the communists and was severely critical of the Congress Party. He was forever championing lost causes! In the clamour made by sabre-rattlers for a tough line against Pakistan, he spoke up for friendship with Pakistan; in the chauvinistic denunciations of Sheikh Abdullah as a pro-Pakistani traitor, he acclaimed Abdullah as a patriot to whom India owed the accession of Kashmir; in an atmosphere fouled by killings and counter-killings in Nagaland, he was the only Indian who spoke up for the Nagas. He was rightly regarded as the conscience-keeper of the nation.

My introduction to JP came through David Astor, the owner-editor of England's prestigious weekly, *The Observer*. Like JP, Astor was a champion of unpopular causes. During the British Raj, he had supported Gandhi and Nehru; after India became free, he became critical of Nehru and lent support to JP. Under the influence of Guy Wint and Ursula Graham Bower, who had lived in Nagaland, he took up the cause of the Nagas and persuaded JP to look into their grievances. At the time, the Indian Army had succeeded in squashing (as it later appeared, only temporarily) Naga insurgency and the Naga militant leader A. Z. Phizo was on the run. I had known Astor since my university days; it was Astor who asked me to call on JP who was then in London.

I went to see JP as I was bidden. He was staying in Brown's Hotel. Brown's, though in fashionable Bond Street, was what might in Indian terms be described as a three-star hotel. JP occupied a small cubicle-sized room above the entrance. I had no difficulty in recognizing him as by now his photographs had appeared in all the papers and he had become a legend. My first impression of him did not change: he was a soft-spoken man of great charm; whether or not a person agreed with him, it was difficult to resist falling for him. I did. He asked me to help him look into the grievances of the Nagas and advise him on the course of action. I was flattered. Although I readily agreed to do so, I confessed that I knew nothing about the Nagas or their problems. I was told that I would be briefed by someone who would come to see me that evening. Perhaps I could give him a drink and a bite.

I was reading Ursula Graham Bower's book on the Nagas when my bell rang. I opened the door. It was a small, pale-skinned man with Mongoloid features, a scraggy goatee, and one side of his face bashed in from eye to cheek. Because of facial paralysis, he had difficulty speaking. It took me some time to realize that this was Phizo. At the time his whereabouts were unknown except to the British authorities, David Astor and to JP. (I was later pleasantly surprised to learn that they were also known to Indian intelligence. Mr Azim Husain, then acting Indian high commissioner, rang me next morning to ask me jocularly why I was entertaining 'our enemies'. It is possible that Azim got the information from my friend Evan Charlton of *The Statesman* who dropped in unexpectedly for a drink.) As I said before, communicating with Phizo was not easy. Besides the impediment in his speech, he was a very bitter man and accused the Indian Army of all manner of diabolical acts—pillage, arson, rape and murder. I refused to believe him. Two days later he made a dramatic appearance at a public meeting and repeated the charges. *The Observer* devoted its front page to 'The Naga Rebellion'.

I called on JP to report my reactions. With him at the time was a tall, austere looking, grey-eyed man in a black coat and a clerical white collar. This was the Reverend Michael Scott. Scott was much loved by Indians for his championship of the blacks against the white racist regime in South Africa. I was somewhat agitated at what I believed to be the utterly baseless charges Phizo had made against our army. They heard me out in patient silence.

Back home in Delhi, I was again drawn into the Naga business. JP handed me a sizeable file containing allegations compiled by Michael Scott from his interviews with the Nagas. I was unable to make sense of them and suspected the atrocity stories to be very exaggerated, and said so to JP. However, by now our intelligence chaps were on my trail. A young IAS officer began to cultivate me and one evening, after grossly flattering me about my eminence as a writer, asked me bluntly whether I could let him see the documents that JP had given me. He followed up the request by suggesting that he could make the deal worth my while. When that did not work, he appealed to my sense of patriotism. In return I quoted E. M. Forster to him: '...if I had to choose between betraying my country and betraying my friend I hope I should have the guts to betray my country.' He was flabbergasted and took his leave. I reported the attempt to bribe me to JP. He simply smiled and said, 'How unnecessary! I have given a copy of the charges to Prime Minister Shastri.'

Not very long afterwards, Michael Scott, the same man our government had lauded for his pro-India role in South Africa, was declared persona non grata by the government because he had taken up a cause which it found inconvenient.

The Naga issue petered out. Plainclothesmen did not find it worth their while to waste time on me. Whenever JP came to Delhi (he usually stayed with J. J. Singh in Friend's Colony) I called on him. I took part in several seminars conducted by him. He made an excellent moderator—he was lucid, utterly objective and spoke in a manner reminiscent of the groves of academe. He had a better mind than any of our politicians, he was a man of impeccable moral character and there was never a breath of scandal about him. He was loved by everyone who knew him, but for some mysterious reason he did not make it to the top. He was neither a mahatma in the Gandhian mould, nor a raja of Nehruvian dimensions. He commanded more affection than awe, more respect than fear. Even his close friends like Minoo Masani spoke of him as 'indecisive'. Compliments paid to him were usually in negative terms: 'He is not assertive enough...he is too gentle...won't hurt a fly...can't tell a lie...trusts everybody...won't let down a friend who's betrayed him.' And so on.

I recall one meeting in Masani's house when he (Masani) was leader of the Swatantra Party and an MP. JP was sharing his analysis of the political scene in the country to an invited group of friends when Maharani Gayatri Devi, still ravishingly beautiful, came in. Seeing the chairs and sofas occupied, she sat down on the carpet beside JP.

JP paused for a long while as if his train of thought had been derailed. And then remarked in his usual soft, monotone voice: 'This indeed is democracy! A maharani sitting at the feet of a commoner.'

I was in Los Angeles in 1965 when the Indo-Pak war broke out. It upset me very much because I had always (as I do today) given top priority to friendship with Pakistan. I never believed in the canards our newspapers published with sickening regularity about Pakistanis wanting to invade India; we were (as we are today) more than twice as powerful on land, sea and air than Pakistan. And having met President Ayub Khan I was convinced that the war could not be of his choosing. I was in a miniscule minority but felt sure that at least one man in India would see my point of view. On my way home, I broke journey at Hong Kong and, knowing that this would be my only chance of communicating with Pakistan, I wrote a letter to President Ayub Khan expressing my sorrow at the turn of events and appealing to him to call for a ceasefire. I also wrote an impassioned letter to JP suggesting that he lead a band of passive resisters, of whom I would be one, to offer satyagraha between the firing lines of the two armies. I arrived back in Bombay during a blackout.

My epistles were treated with the contempt they deserved. From my friend Manzur Qadir, who had been Pakistan's foreign minister, I learned that President Ayub was vastly amused by my letter. Being laughed at did not bother me very much but to find that JP was not even amused hurt me deeply. He supported the Indian government's view that Pakistan had provoked the war and deserved what it was getting.

I should have known better. JP was not a pacifist. His main point of disagreement with Gandhi was that he believed in the legitimacy of the use of force in certain circumstances. It was his gentle manner, his sense of fairness, the ability to see an adversary's point of view, his close association with Vinoba Bhave's Bhoodan and Sarvodaya which had beguiled me into believing that he, like Gandhi and Vinoba Bhave, regarded ahimsa as paramo dharma. He did not. He was a krantikari.

I came closer to JP during the Bihar famine of 1967. Without warning I descended on him at Patna and announced that I had come to work as his private secretary. He was embarrassed. He did not want me as his secretary and did not really know how to make use of me. However, I stuck to him, saw him every day in his modest house in Kadam Kuan—the ground floor and courtyard had been given over to a school, two sparsely furnished rooms on the first floor were all that he and his wife Prabhavati had kept for themselves. Ultimately he decided that I should see things for myself, write about them and thereby generate sympathy and money for the work his organization was doing.

I accompanied JP and his wife to his farm in Sokhodeora, a few hours' drive from Patna. This was the first time I saw the two at close quarters over a stretch of days. They were said never to have known physical intimacy. Under Gandhi's baleful influence Prabhavati, without as much as consulting her husband, had taken a vow of celibacy. Somehow I refused to believe that this vow had been strictly observed. They had been together before Prabhavati had met Gandhi at Wardha. JP had been a strapping youth and made no secret of his liking for good-looking women. Even in her late fifties Prabhavati was a most attractive woman: fair, petite, animated and with a mischievous twinkle in her eyes. However, whether or not there was any truth to the notion that their relationship was purely platonic, they were very close to each other. When they were in company, they usually spoke to each other in their Bhojpuri dialect as if they wanted to be only with each other and exclude everyone else. She watched over him like a tigress watches her cubs. He was already in indifferent health: diabetic and with an enlarged prostate. He also suffered from chronic constipation. We had to stop many times for JP to empty his bladder. Prabhavati was always plying him with pills for something or the other, getting water or tea out of different thermos flasks she carried in a hamper, mixing Isabgol with his cup of milk, harar behera in his butter milk: it was ayurvedic, unani, homeopathic, allopathic—everything. But above all it was the loving, fussing Prabhavati who gave JP the real touch of healing.

At Sokhodeora I was with JP from dawn to well after sunset. Sarvodaya workers and villagers would assemble round his little cottage in the early hours. He would hear them out and speak to them till Prabhavati summoned him indoors for his breakfast of buttermilk and fruit. He then left the ashram by car or jeep to tour afflicted villages. Everywhere it was the same story—wells dried up, granaries empty and hungry children wailing for food. He gave what he brought with him, listened to their tales of woe by the hour. I found it very exasperating to see a man of action, as true a karmayogi as I had ever met, wasting his time listening to old women's woes. What an efficient executive would have done in five minutes, JP took fifty minutes to do. It drastically reduced his effectiveness. But he was beyond changing. He returned to Sokhodeora long after the scheduled time for lunch. There were always more people waiting to see him. He could not hurt them by refusing to listen to them. It went on till the irate Prabhavati drove them off without ceremony and took her husband indoors. The nagging went on through the meal till he wearily retired for his siesta. Prabhavati snoozed in a chair outside to prevent anyone disturbing her husband.

The afternoon was spent in the same way: touring villages, talking to villagers, giving them succour in cash, grain and words of hope. Then back to Sokhodeora to instruct Sarvodaya workers. It was only after dark that the two were left alone.

And these were the most rewarding moments of my all-too-brief association with them. We sat round a table with a hurricane lantern, the stars twinkling overhead. Jackals wailed in the wilderness and their howls mingled with the weird cries of villagers driving them off their fields. I had my Scotch—neither JP nor his wife had any hang-ups about what anyone ate or drank—and JP reminisced about the past for my benefit. There was a brief interruption to listen to the news and to eat the vegetarian meal that Prabhavati had cooked for us. They invariably walked to my shack, saw that my bed had been made, the mosquito net hung, and a flask of drinking water put on the table. By 10 p.m. Sokhodeora was fast asleep save for the dogs baying at a late moon and the villagers shouting abuse at wild pigs that raided their fields.

It was during these evening sessions by the light of the hurricane lantern that I got an inkling of the strained relations between JP and Indira Gandhi. JP was virtually the only leader of national importance who was devoting himself to famine relief operations; his popularity among the people was ever increasing. The state government was very grudging in its appreciation of his work. Mrs Gandhi visited Bihar twice and both times met JP. Twice she promised to appeal to the people to help JP and both times did not do so. Did she resent JP's growing popularity? JP did not say so in so many words but the number of times he brought up the subject left little doubt in my mind that he thought so. (This was confirmed years later, when JP openly broke with her and launched his Total Revolution. In an interview I had with her, she lashed out: 'Who made JP a leader? What following has he in the country? It is you newspaper people who exaggerate his popularity...')

My contribution to relieve the hunger of the people of Bihar did not go beyond writing a series of sob-stuff articles for *The Statesman* which brought in some cheques to JP's organization. But the contact made in those few days lasted many years. I even toyed with the idea of working on his biography and at his insistence wrote to Dr H. Passim, an American professor who had borrowed JP's papers but had done nothing about them. The project came to an end with a brusque and rude note from Passim saying that the papers were his private property and I should stop pestering him. Apparently Passim was waiting for the day when JP became prime minister of India when his biography would ensure Passim handsome royalties.

I resumed contact with JP when he launched his Total Revolution. Though at the time I held no brief for Mrs Gandhi or her government, I made no secret of my total disagreement with a revolution which took the form of gheraoing (and at times assaulting) elected members of legislatures. But so unpopular had Mrs Gandhi's government become that JP's movement gathered strength. When he came to Bombay, I had the privilege of bringing him and Prabhavati for lunch to meet editors of the *Times of India* group of papers and journals. He looked very sick and Prabhavati had her usual hawkish eye on what he ate and how long he stayed. The next day I travelled with him from Bombay to Poona. Prabhavati was not with us so I had him all to myself and took the opportunity to ask him about his past. We were constantly interrupted by admirers coming to greet him. At every station there were crowds to pay him homage. By the time we reached Poona, he was exhausted by his visitors and by my ceaseless stream of questions. But for me it was a most rewarding train journey. He spoke with great candour, even naming girls with whom he had had affairs in his younger days. He attributed his poor health to the rough time he had had in the United States and the Indian doctor who had performed a very clumsy operation to remove his tonsils.

The gathering he addressed in Poona that afternoon was not as large as the one he had addressed in Bombay two days earlier. But it was large enough—about 60,000 people. I had no doubt that this movement was assuming the dimensions of a revolt. I wrote about 'The Total Revolution' for the *New York Times,* criticizing it as anti-democratic. JP was very hurt and wrote me a long letter saying that I had misunderstood the purpose of the movement, which was aimed at wiping out the corruption that had fouled our democratic institutions. I published his letter in the *Illustrated Weekly of India* which I was then editing. But a breach had been made in our relationship which was not to be healed. I wrote to (and even personally warned) Mrs Gandhi that although I disapproved of JP's movement, she was underestimating the strength that JP had gathered. It was then that she made the comment questioning JP's popularity that I have quoted earlier.

I saw JP lead the massive procession in Delhi on 6 March 1975, with Charan Singh, Atal Behari Vajpayee, Badal, Chandra Shekhar and many other leaders in tow. Among the hundreds of thousands of marchers, I had no difficulty in identifying RSS volunteers and the Jan Sangh. They were among the cheerleaders and slogan-makers: 'Desh ka neta? Jayaprakash. Andher ka roshan? Jayaprakash. Sab mil key bolo. Jayaprakash.' Anyone gifted with a little foresight could have seen the shape of things to come. Indira Gandhi and JP, who should have been on the same side, fighting against this force of resurgent fascism, were busy destroying each other; the only outcome of their conflict would be chaos and the only beneficiaries of the chaos would be either these backward-looking elements of Hindu communal forces or the communists.

When Mrs Gandhi declared the Emergency I was not sure on whose side I was. While I strongly resented the arrests and detention without trial of thousands of men and women and the muzzling of the press, I felt equally strongly that JP's Total Revolution had richly contributed to bringing us to this sorry state of affairs. The fact that there was hardly a murmur of protest—on the contrary, a vast majority of the people sighed with relief—was ample proof that the people did not regard the Emergency as an evil (as it was later made out to be). Schools, factories and shops opened; strikes, lockouts, gheraos, hooliganism came to an end. I was however saddened by the fact that a saintly, lovable man like JP who was in poor health had been locked up. I was also conscious of his feeling that in siding with Indira Gandhi I had let him down. However, when he was brought to Jaslok Hospital in Bombay, I went to see him. Dr S. Mehta, who was treating him, did not give him many days. I was not able to have the heart-to-heart talk with him which I desperately wanted. He was obviously very hurt but being assured of my affection and being a gentleman he agreed to see me. 'I will ring you up when I am better,' he promised both the times I called on him. He never did.

And then he rose from his sickbed to lead the Janata to victory and be acclaimed as the Lok Nayak and the saviour of the nation. I did not see him in that light. And, being temperamentally incapable of seeking contact with people in power, kept my distance.

I do not know how history will judge JP. All I know is that most of the people who today are heaping adjectives of praise on him thought little of him before. They exploited him, rode his bandwagon to power without having the slightest regard or affection for him. He is a good man, an honest man, an able man and a brave man. Leadership has been thrust upon him by men who were neither honest nor able nor brave so that they could become leaders themselves.

SPIRITUAL LEADERS

ACHARYA RAJNEESH
(1931–1990)

I was truly grieved to hear of the passing of the Acharya Rajneesh. In my opinion, for whatever it is worth, he was the most original thinker that India has produced: the most erudite, the most clear-headed and the most innovative. And in addition, he had an inborn gift for words, spoken and written. We will not see the likes of him for decades to come.

Rajneesh's gimmickry created a totally false picture of him as a person and a philosopher. High living with fleets of Rolls-Royces, free sex, frequent changes of titles: Acharya to Bhagwan to Maitreyi the Buddha to Osho. All that is of little consequence. He has to be judged as a thinker, and as a thinker he will rank among giants.

Although dubbed a Godman, Rajneesh did not believe in God. 'God,' he wrote 'is the most meaningless word in the human language.' Neither Jain Mahavira nor Buddha believed in God: only some of their stupid followers do so. Rajneesh did not believe in any religion. 'All the religions have reduced humanity into beggars. They call it prayer, they call it worship—beautiful names to hide an ugly reality,' he wrote. 'All beliefs are blind, all beliefs are false. They do not let you grow up, they only help you kneel down like a slave before dead statues, rotten scriptures, primitive philosophies,' he wrote. He did not believe in life before death or life after death. 'This is the only planet we have, this is the only time we have, and this is the only life we have,' he wrote. 'So make the best of it, get the most you can out of it.'

It is impossible to do justice to this great man in a few words. I would exhort my readers to read his sermons now printed in hundreds of books. With the going of Rajneesh, India has lost one of its greatest sons. India's loss will be shared by all who have an open mind throughout the world.

The only time I met Acharya Rajneesh, I asked him about death. There was nothing very profound about our dialogue as it did not go beyond the restatement of platitudes—knowing death is inevitable, why do we fear it? Is there any way of overcoming the phobia? Do we know anything about what happens to us after we die? And so on. The Acharya has now put all his thoughts on the subject together in a small 100-page booklet entitled *Death: The Greatest Fiction*. For once, I am disappointed with his treatment of a serious and disturbing topic. Death is not a fiction; it is a profound reality, more real than anything in life.

The Acharya has an inimitable style of simplifying the most abstruse themes and illustrating them with pithy anecdotes. The offhand way in which he mocks the pretensions of prophets and philosophers is refreshing. But this time, he is unconvincing.

He starts his discourse by narrating his first exposure to death. He was only seven years old. He was taking his sick grandfather to hospital in a bullock cart with only his grandmother and the cart driver as his companions. On the way, the grandfather, barely fifty, gave up the ghost. His last words were: 'My Lord, this life you have given me, I surrender it back to you with my thanks.' None in the cart shed a tear. When told that her old man had stopped breathing, the grandmother reassured Rajneesh, 'That's perfectly okay, as he had lived enough; there is no need to ask for more... Remember, because these are the moments not to be forgotten, never ask for more. What is, is enough.' Then she burst into a song.

Acharya assures us that death is not the end of a man's journey but a door to God. The death of a loved one certainly creates a vacuum but since life itself is meaningless, there is nothing to mourn about. One should not fear death but regard it as a long, relaxed sleep from which you wake up to a brighter dawn. He writes: 'People who are afraid of death cannot relax in sleep, because sleep is also a very small death that comes every day. People who are afraid of death are also afraid of love, because love is a death. People who are afraid of death become afraid of all orgasmic experiences, because in each orgasm, the ego dies.'

I am out of my depth. I am not afraid of love; I also regard an orgasm as the ultimate in physical exaltation. Yet I fear death.

The Acharya proceeds to make further assertions, which leave me flabbergasted. He asserts that a dying man sees in a flash his entire life. But if he has unfulfilled desires, they will deckle his future life. 'So what you do at the moment of your death determines how your birth is going to be,' he says.

I go along with Rajneesh when he says that life should be lived as intensely as possible (though this would seem to contradict his earlier statement that life is meaningless), but I fail to comprehend what he means when he says, 'In my religion, death is celebrated because there is no death. It is only an entry into another life.' He faults the Hebraic family of religions (Judaism, Christianity and Islam) for believing in only one life. That, according to him, is why Westerners who subscribe to these religions are always in a hurry to get things done and have never grasped the concept of meditation. Whereas Indians, because they believe in rebirth, don't feel the pressure of time, are non-achievers but meditative.

'Religion only has validity because of death,' says Acharya Rajneesh. 'If there is no death, nobody would have bothered about religion at all.' He is right on track there. But why then is religion, in all its spurious manifestations, more in evidence in India where the vast majority believe in reincarnation than elsewhere? What evidence has he for saying that death is a 'beautiful sleep, a dreamless sleep, a sleep that is needed for you to enter into another body, silently and peacefully'? He goes on to reassert that 'those who die unconsciously will be born on some other planet, in some other womb'.

It is not fair on the part of the Acharya to ask us to take his word and accept the theory of transmigration of souls. 'It is my experience... When I say that the soul transmigrates, to me it is an experience. I remember my past lives. I have transmigrated; there is no question of doubt for me, but I am not saying this for you to believe it.' He talks of deja vu—an experience some people have when they visit a new place. They feel they have been there before because they have in fact done so in their previous lives. No sceptic or rationalist will buy this argument.

I go along with the Acharya in his general approach to life. He says: 'These are the 'three Ls' of my philosophy: life, love, laughter. Life is only a seed, love is a flower, laughter is a fragrance. Just to be born is not enough, one has to learn the art of living; that is the A of meditation. Then one has to learn the art of loving; that is the B of meditation. And then one has to learn the art of laughing; that is the C of meditation. And meditation has only three letters: A, B, C.'

It is difficult to accept the Acharya's views on death. Having allowed himself to become a Bhagwan, he has forfeited the right to say, 'I do not know.' Nobody, not even Bhagwan Rajneesh, knows what happens to us when we die. And as long as we do not know, we will continue to dread it.

U. G. KRISHNAMURTI
(1918–2007)

Not Jiddu Krishnamurti but Uppaluri Gopala Krishnamurti, known to his friends and admirers as UG. Besides having the same surname there are other things about UG that make you think of Jiddu. He is handsome, into discourses and dialogues, writes books and has a philosophy to propound. He is not as well known as Jiddu, hence a short biographical sketch may be useful.

U. G. Krishnamurti was born in Masulipatam on 9 July 1918, the first and only child of his mother, who died of puerperal fever a week after giving birth to him. His father remarried and went out of his life. He was brought up by his maternal grandparents, both of whom were ardent theosophists, knew Annie Besant and Jiddu Krishnamurti. UG spent his childhood years around Adyar, the centre of theosophy. He also travelled all over India and spent seven years in the Himalayas studying yoga under Swami Sivananda. He rejected yoga and asceticism and in his mid-twenties took a wife. Although he felt that marriage had been 'the biggest mistake' of his life, he remained married for seventeen years and sired four children. He migrated to the United States, found a job for his wife and then abandoned his family. He eked out a miserable living giving lectures on theosophy and Indian cooking. From the States he went to London, then Paris and ultimately to Geneva to have himself repatriated to India. He had no money to pay for his passage. At the consulate where he narrated his dismal tale of failure, the lady secretary who was translating his narration was fascinated by his life story and offered to house him. The lady, Valentine deKerven, was in her early sixties. UG was seventeen years her junior. They have lived together ever since and have travelled extensively over the world. She is now in her eighties; he is seventy.

It had been predicted in his horoscope that his forty-ninth birthday would be a crucial turning point. It was on that day he heard Jiddu Krishnamurti speak at the Swiss village Saanen where Valentine and he had bought a chalet. On his way back from the lecture he sat by a stream and pondered. He came to the conclusion that: 'There is no such thing as spiritual or psychological enlightenment because there is no such thing as spirit or psyche at all. I have been a damn fool all my life, searching for something which does not exist. My search is at an end.'

The change in outlook was accompanied by a change in his physiognomy. 'The hands and forearms changed their structure, so that now his hands face backward instead of to the sides. His body is now hermaphroditic, a perfect union of animus-anima, and enjoys a sexuality the likes of which we can only guess. His right side responds to women, his left more to men.' UG, whose teaching was described as destructive as Shiva in his role of a destroyer became veritably an ardhanari.

I am not sure if I have caught his message right. In the compilation of his interviews, entitled *Mind is a Myth: Disquieting Conversations with the Man called U. G.*, Terry Newland gives a summary of the many things UG stands for:

> Making love is war; cause and effect is the shibboleth of confused minds; yoga and health foods destroy the body; the body and not the soul is immortal; there is no Communism in Russia, no freedom in America, and no spirituality in India; service to mankind is utter selfishness; Jesus was another misguided Jew and the Buddha was a crackpot; mutual terror, not love, will save mankind; attending church and going to the bar for a drink are identical; there is nothing inside you but fear; communication is impossible between human beings; God, love, happiness, the unconscious, death, reincarnation and the soul are non-existent figments of our rich imagination; Freud is the fraud of the 20th century, while J. Krishnamurti its greatest phoney.

I have read and reviewed *Mind is a Myth*. I share many of his disbeliefs—in God, prophets, scriptures and organized religion—distrust of godmen and utter contempt for their gullible followers. What irritates UG is that despite his denunciation of religion and godmen, a growing number of religiously inclined men and women hang on to every word he says and regard him as a modern messiah.

UG happened to be in Delhi, staying with Frank Noronha of the Indian Information Service who first introduced me to his writings. I went to see him to discuss matters like, if not God, then who, the purpose of life, the phenomenon of death and why so many people continue to believe in life after death. As I shook hands with him, there was a long distance call from Bombay. It was somebody speaking on behalf of Parveen Babi who had attached herself to UG. He was pretty rough in his reply: 'No, I cannot come to Bombay and will be in Bangalore tomorrow; don't waste your time and money coming to see me; I can do nothing.'

He brushed his silver-grey locks and took his seat. He is an incredibly handsome man and looks closer to fifty than the actual seventy-two. A movie camera recorded every word that passed between us. Actually, it was more of a monologue than a dialogue. After saying that he had nothing to say, no message to give but would only respond to questions put to him he proceeded to deliver a long oration denouncing Sai Baba, Rajneesh and their followers. It was a good fifteen minutes later that I was able to butt in with a question: 'I go along with you in rejecting accepted beliefs, but then how do we explain existence?' He discarded my question as irrelevant as it was based on the assumption that everything had a cause; according to him the cause and effect theory was fallacious and operated within the religious framework. I was not convinced. It was the same about death. While he agreed with me that it was a full stop to consciousness, he holds that our atomic existence continued in a different shape. That also I could not comprehend. I gave up the battle—he had too many words in his armoury for me to contend with.

'Where does he get all this energy from?' I asked Noronha as he drove me back home. 'Not from what he eats,' he replied. 'All he takes is a spoonful or two of cream mixed with mashed rice twice a day. No bread, no meat or vegetables; no tea, coffee or milk. He seems to be able to do with very little food and sleep. He is up most of the day and night and only takes an occasional catnap. The rest of the time he is talking or reading.' That is probably what gives UG the aura of godliness; he has spiritual energy of demonic proportions.

Spiritual Leaders

GURU NANAK
(1469–1539)

The Sikhs are celebrating the 500th birthday of the founder of their faith. For the last ten years they have been planning for these celebrations—to raise new universities, colleges, hospitals and schools; publish literature; arrange seminars and lectures; organize the non-stop chanting of hymns; take out massive processions; entertain their friends at tea parties and banquets. Some of these schemes have been carried out, many will remain unfulfilled. And almost everyone will feel that much more could have been achieved if only... The chief cause of Sikh frustration comes from the feeling that the message of Nanak was not really conveyed to non-Sikhs and that the participation of other communities was merely symbolic, a gesture of goodwill. No more.

The sense of frustration is inevitable. People are not really interested in faiths and practices other than their own. It is also an error to believe that processions, meetings, lectures and literature influence people's minds. They have little or no impact. It is not the excellence of the life of a prophet or his teaching that matters (lives of prophets as well as their messages have a quality of sameness); what matters is the way of life and conduct of those that profess to be his followers. In the final analysis, Guru Nanak will be judged not by what he did and said but by what his followers today do, say, and the way they behave towards other people.

There is an element of simplicity in Nanak's life and teachings. His life was an example of Thomas Paine's precepts: 'The world is my country, all mankind are my brethren, and to do good is my religion.' His teachings could be summed up in two words—work and worship—in that order. Only he put it all in very beautiful poetry. If the Sikhs really wish to pay homage to their founder-Guru and impress their non-Sikh friends with his greatness, they have an excellent opportunity to do so. We are the world's poorest country with the highest proportion of non-workers—beggars, sadhus, yogis. This places a bigger burden on those who, like the Sikhs, believe in the adage 'Work is worship'. Work harder so that there is something to spare for the needy. Also in recent years the atmosphere in our country has been fouled by communal passions. Nanak made the bringing of Hindus and Muslims together the chief mission of his life. What greater way is there to do honour to his memory than by continuing that crusade? Sikhs could play a unique role in organizing corps of volunteers in our towns and villages dedicated to the task of keeping the peace, of fostering fraternal relations between communities and by making their gurdwaras sanctuaries for victims of communal frenzy. Nanak became the king of holy men (Shah fakir) because the Hindus recognized him as their guru, the Mussalmans as their pir. Nanak's Sikhs could emulate his example. Let me coin a doggerel for them:

Singh Soorma Shah Sardar Hindu ka dost, Mussulman ka yaar.

MOTHER TERESA
(1910–1997)

Ask anyone 'Who is the best-known and best-loved citizen of Calcutta?' Nine persons out of ten will answer: 'Mother Teresa.' The clue to how a white foreigner came to be loved by a people notorious for their xenophobia can be found beside the temple of Kali.

Kali being the patron Goddess of Bengal, during her puja festival in autumn the number of worshippers runs into millions. Rest houses for pilgrims (dharamshalas) built in the vicinity of the temple are full. At other times they remain empty. One adjoining the temple wall consists of two spacious dormitories. In 1952, the Corporation handed it over to Mother Teresa. She put up her sign board: 'Nirmal Hriday—(Sacred Heart) Home for Dying Destitutes.'

There was an uproar. Orthodox Hindus were outraged that a Catholic institution was being established within the temple complex. The four hundred Brahmin priests attached to the temple organized demonstrations and yelled slogans demanding that the Catholics be thrown out. Mother Teresa told me the story herself. 'One day I went out and spoke to them. "If you want to kill me, kill me. But do not disturb the inmates. Let them die in peace." That silenced them. Then one of the priests staggered in. He was an advanced case of galloping phthisis. We looked after him till he died. It changed their attitude towards us. Today we are the best of friends. They give us all the help they can.' One of Mother Teresa's admirers told me the sequel. Later one day another priest entered the home and protracted himself at the feet of Mother Teresa. 'For thirty years I have served Goddess Kali in her temple,' he said. 'Now the Goddess stands before me.'

Only the stout-hearted can take the Home for Dying Destitutes in their stride. In both the dormitories, extending from one to the other, are three rows of low steel framed beds with just enough room between them for a person to stand. There is an image of the Virgin above the entrance with a dim light that burns at all hours. All that relieves the monotony of the high walls are placards with Christian motifs and metal hooks from which ropes are stretched across the rooms, to hang bottles of saline solution with tubes stuck into the patients. The passage between the men's and the women's dormitories is used as a kitchen. A small platform above the kitchen serves as the office. It has a single chair and a table with two registers to record admissions and deaths. When I visited the place there were seventy-seven men and ninety-three women being tended to by five nuns and brothers.

Death spread a pall of gloom in the dimly lit dormitories. Emaciated men and women sat on their beds, staring vacantly at each other or lying wrapped like corpses in dark brown shrouds. Before proceeding on her rounds Mother Teresa genuflected and crossed herself in front of a diminutive figurine of the Virgin. The person in the first bed was covered from head to foot. Mother Teresa raised a corner of his blanket. It was a young man wasted by consumption and gasping for breath. She felt his fevered temples. 'He won't last many hours,' she remarked without any emotion as she covered his face again. The next one was a man in his sixties. He introduced himself in English, 'I am Valdin Noronha, sea man from Goa,' and exposed a misshapen foot swollen with yellow-green pus. 'A truck ran over it,' he explained. 'They kept me in the hospital for three months and then threw me out. I have nowhere to go. No relatives, no friends, no one in the world.' Mother Teresa ran her hand gently over his deformed foot and spindly leg. 'Gangrene! They should have amputated it from here,' she said in a matter of fact tone, tapping the man's knee. The next one was a boy of five with a head like an oversize football. He clutched Mother Teresa's sari and begged for a bidi. Mother Teresa patted his face and told him that he was too young to smoke. Beside him was another boy of the same age whose body had been badly burnt; he was paralysed from his waist downwards. He was in agony and screamed each time the nun tried to give him an injection. Mother Teresa tried to reason with the boy but failed. 'Leave him alone,' she said to the nun. 'It won't help very much.' And so we went from one bed to another. Mother Teresa talked to everyone who could talk, patted their foreheads, ruffled their hair, examined their sores and commiserated with them. She had no tears left in her, but her compassion was boundless. The only message of cheer she had for those without hope was in Bengali:

Bhogoban acchen—there is God.

We passed the kitchen and came into the women's dormitory. An Anglo-Indian woman in European dress who had just been brought in was lying on the floor shivering as in a bout of malaria. Mother Teresa asked her why she had not gone to hospital. The woman explained that she lived alone, had no one to look after her and begged to be given a bed. 'Yes dear, we'll get you one as soon as one is available,' answered Mother Teresa as she got a blanket and spread it over a woman with sunken eyes and a gurgling in her throat. Mother Teresa stared at her for some time and told me, 'She was brought in only last night, she will be gone very soon.' We went through rows of old women with shaved heads and sunken eyes too tired to smile or talk. One of the nurses was herself faceless—her nose, cheeks and lips were blown up by an exploding petromax lamp leaving her with only eyes and teeth. She too had come to die but lived to serve the dying. There were two others, a boy and a girl, who were likewise rescued from the jaws of death and now work in the house. When we turned back, Mother Teresa again stopped to look at the woman in the corner. Her gurgles had stopped and she seemed to be sleeping peacefully, Mother Teresa felt her forehead and then her pulse. 'She is dead,' she announced in a flat voice. 'Sister, put her in the morgue.' Two nuns lifted the body and took it out. The bed was remade and the Anglo-Indian woman put in her place. I saw the latest entry being made in the register. Name: Shanti Devi. Religion: Hindu. Date and Time of death: 11.30 a.m. 20 December 1973. Shanti Devi was the 3,522nd person to have died in the Sacred Heart Home for the Destitutes. On an average one person dies in the home every twenty-four hours. Of the 29,000 destitutes who came to her, half have died in this place. Mother Teresa has set up similar homes for the dying destitute in other Indian cities.

Malcom Muggeridge in his book *Something Beautiful for God* records a miracle that he witnessed when he came to make a film on Mother Teresa for the BBC. His cameraman was of the opinion that there was not sufficient light in the dormitories and a film he had shot in similar light earlier had been a total loss. He took shots of the building from the outside and the sunlit courtyard. Some film was left so he decided to take a chance and shot the rest indoors. When the film was developed, the scenes in the dormitories were found to be clearer than those taken in sunlight. I asked Mother Teresa if this was true. She replied, 'But of course! Such things happen all the time.' And with increasing intensity of voice, 'Every day, every hour, every single minute, God manifests Himself in some miracle.'

When I was asked to do a profile of Mother Teresa for the *New York Times*, I wrote to her seeking permission to call on her. Having got it, I spent three days with her, from the early hours of the morning to late at night. Nothing in my journalistic career has remained as sharply etched in my memory as those three days with her in Calcutta.

I asked her how she got the money to run her world-wide organization. She replied: 'It comes, money is no great problem. God gives through his people. We have never been short of money. It is more important to get people involved, to make them realize that the sick, old and hungry are their brothers, no? When you write about me, I hope you will capitalize that.' When she started her first school in the slums, all she had was five rupees. But as people came to know what she was doing, they brought things and money. 'It was all divine providence,' she said and narrated some miracles. Once, in winter, they had run out of quilts. The nuns found the sheets but there was no cotton to stuff in them. Mother Teresa got her pillow and just as she was about to rip it open the bell rang. Somebody who was leaving Calcutta for a posting abroad had come to leave his quilts and mattresses with Mother Teresa. On another occasion when they had run out of rice, a lady who had never been to them before brought a bag of rice. Out of curiosity they measured the amount with the tin cup they used for measuring daily rations. It happened to be exactly the quantity they required. 'When I told the lady that, she broke down and cried…to realize that God had used her as an instrument of His will was too much for her.' That afternoon I was with Mother Teresa on a 'begging mission'. We went to call on the manager of a biscuit factory, 'They always give us broken biscuits they cannot sell. The sick like broken biscuits,' she informed me. Mr Jyoti Mukherjee, the young manager of the firm, came out to receive her and escorted us to his teak-wood panelled, air conditioned office. Mother Teresa began by thanking him for what he had done in the past and continued, 'You must have lots of problems. Everything is in short supply: flour, butter, sugar, no?' It was evident that Mr Mukherjee's speech had been taken out of his mouth. 'Yes,' he agreed, 'we are not producing anything like we did last year.'

Mother Teresa went on: 'It must be more difficult for well-to-do people of the middle class. We poor people can beg, they are too ashamed to beg, no?' I could see Mukherjee's defences crumble. He looked unhappy with himself. Mother Teresa continued in a gentler tone. 'Why all these shortages? Why are prices going up? Please tell me. I do not understand politics.' Jyoti Mukherjee became expansive and told her of union troubles, strikes, lockouts. 'Thank God!' exclaimed Mother Teresa. 'We only work for God; there are no unions.' She proceeded to elucidate on the hard times. 'The other day we picked up a hungry beggar. He had not eaten for many weeks. When we brought him a plate of rice he said, "I haven't seen rice for many weeks; let me look at it!" And he died staring at that plateful of rice.' Mr Mukherjee picked up his phone and rang up the storekeeper for forty large tins of broken biscuits to be delivered to Mother Teresa.

On my way back, Mother Teresa dropped me at the Dum Dum Airport. As I was about to take leave of her, she said, 'So?' She wanted to know if I had anything else to ask her.

'Tell me, how can you touch people with loathsome diseases like leprosy and gangrene? Aren't you revolted by people filthy with dysentery and cholera vomit?'

'I see Jesus in every human being,' Mother Teresa replied. 'I say to myself, this is hungry Jesus. I must feed him. This is sick Jesus. This one has gangrene, dysentery or cholera. I must wash him and tend to him.'

I wrote a humble tribute to her for the *New York Times* and put her on the cover of the *Illustrated Weekly*. Till then, she was little known outside Calcutta; after that, more people got to know about her work. She sent me a short note of thanks, which I have in a silver frame in Kasauli. It is among my most valued possessions. It says: 'I am told you do not believe in God. I send you God's blessings.'

KABIR

(1440–1518)

Without doubt the most popular saint-poet of northern India was, and is, Bhakta Kabir. Almost everyone, be she/he Hindu, Muslim, Sikh or Christian, educated or unlettered, rich or poor, will know a doha or two by Kabir by heart. And yet we have no definitive biography of the man. The popular cherished belief is that he was born in Benaras, of Brahmin parents, but was adopted and raised by a Muslim weaver's family. I find that hard to accept. My own reading is that he was the son of a Muslim weaver who was influenced by the teachings of Hindu bhaktas and rose above considerations of caste and religion. In his writings, he always referred to himself as a julaha (weaver).

There are two distinct compilations of Kabir's poems, his granthavali which is an anthology of his dohas known by rote by millions of Indians, and his slokas, incorporated by Guru Arjan in the Adi Granth, that are known to those familiar with the Sikh scriptures. Though the message that comes through is the same, the two read quite differently. While the former have been rendered into English many times, the latter have only been rendered by scholars like Max Arthur, Macauliffe, Manmohan Singh, Gopal Singh and Talib as parts of their translations of the Adi Granth. For the first time, the Kabir of the Sikh scriptures has been published in translation in a separate book, *So Spake Kabira*, by Kartar Singh Duggal. He has taken the trouble to render Kabir in poetic form and his translation makes pleasanter reading than the translations of his predecessors. If he had presented the opening lines of the slokas in Roman script, it would have made identification easier.

Duggal is among the top three or four writers in Punjabi; his output of novels, short stories and poems would fill a couple of shelves of a library. Rather late in life he realized that Punjabi could take him only that far but no further. So he switched to English. He is equally prolific in both languages. I can't think of another person who could have done more justice to Kabir than Duggal. He is a devout Sikh, his wife is Muslim.

Kabir was by no means the founder of the Bhakti movement as stated by Duggal. The movement had started more than a couple of centuries earlier in Tamil Nadu and spread northwards. A popular couplet describes its advent and increase:

> *Bhakti Dravid oopjee, uttar Ramanand*
> *pargat kiyo Kabir nay sapt dweep nav khand.*

> Bhakti was born in Dravidian country; brought north by Ramanand; Kabir spread it over the seven seas and nine continents.

Kabir's message in the simplest words is the total rejection of religious bigotry of any kind. He mocked the pretensions of mullahs and pandits with equal relish, pointed out the futility of erecting mosques and temples for a God who is all-pervasive, and scorned the arrogance of the rich and the powerful who, like the poor and the destitute, must go into oblivion. He asked, 'What is the point of putting bricks and stones together or raising a minaret for the mullah to shout the call for prayer? Has God become hard of hearing? And why bother about the mighty and the rich? They are no better than the date palm which casts a very small shade for the weary traveller and its fruit is far beyond reach.' Kabir accepted the Semitic version of the origin of life:

> *Avval Allah noor upaaya*
> *Qudrat ke sab bandey*
> *Ek noor to sab jag upjea*
> *Kaun bhaley kaun mandey.*

> At first God created light,
> We are creatures of nature;
> From one light came the entire world
> Who then is high and who is low?

He summed up what the aim of life should be in four memorable lines:

> *Jab ham aaye jagat mein,*
> *Jag hassa ham roey;*

Aisee karnee kar chalen
Jab ham jaayen jagat say
Ham hassein jag roey.

When I was born
everyone rejoiced but I did cry
Fill your life with such deeds that
When you die
You have a smile on your lips while others cry.

BHAI VIR SINGH
(1872–1957)

The last time I met Bhai Vir Singh was three months ago in Amritsar. He was a sick man under the care of nurses and doctors. His bed and sitting rooms were heated by Canadian stoves and a constant watch was kept on the temperature. The doctor had forbidden him to work or receive visitors. There were only a few exceptions to this rule; among them were younger writers for whom Vir Singh always had a sort of personal regard. He walked into the sitting room slowly but unescorted. I touched his feet; he put his frail hand on my shoulder and asked me to sit down beside him. He enquired about my children for he always loved children. He spoke with effort and had to pause for breath after each sentence and then became silent. He was never a man of too many words and the custom of the circle around him was to sit in silence and meditate. After ten minutes he looked up and smiled. I knew I was expected to leave.

'When will you be going to the hills?' I asked.

He raised one hand in a gesture of resignation and answered: 'Who knows!'

LONGING FOR TOUCH

I got up and once more touched his feet. This time he took my hands in his—his soft, warm hands which had the ability to stir deep emotions and without rhyme or reason bring tears to one's eyes.

'Give my love to your daughter. God bless you.'

I hurried out of the room. It was obvious that his time was fast running out. He did not seem concerned because to him life had meant reading and writing and the doctor had forbidden him both. And he was of the philosophical mould, those who take both life and death in their stride. I left his house but the memory of his touch lingered for a long time. Therein lay the secret of one of the dominant themes in his poems—a sensuous longing for physical contact with God in the tradition of the Vaishnava and Sufi writers, a sort of mystic belief that the touch would evoke the angelic in man and, as a philosopher's stone, transmute dross to gold.

> You struck the chords
> And I burst into music
> Like a harp attuned.
> You forsook me
> And I feel silent
> As one stricken dumb.
> Thy hand hath the magic touch.
> It makes the living come to Life.

The 'touch' had mystical significance for Vir Singh. It occurs often in his writing:

> In a dream You came to me
> I leapt to hold You in my embrace;
> It was but a fantasy I could not hold
> And my arms ached with longing.
> Then I rushed to clasp Your feet
> To lay my head thereon:
> Even these I could not reach
> For You were high and I was low.

TWENTY YEARS AFTER

This last meeting was a strange contrast with the first, more than twenty years ago. Vir Singh was then over sixty and a legendary figure. He had become one in his twenties with the publication of his first novel, *Sundari*. It is hard to believe that a man like him should have become the subject of such fierce controversy among a people who admired his writing, were grateful to him for what he was doing, and above all, who never joined a faction against another or said one word of disparagement about anyone. The main criticism was against his allowing people to worship him—which indeed thousands did—and his being surrounded by a circle which consisted largely of the wealthier sections of Sikh society. Young people were highly critical of him on these scores; I counted myself among them and not only refused to touch his feet but made fun of people who made obeisance before him. Yet I lived to make my obeisance, touch his feet and give him the respect I would give no other living man.

A man of Vir Singh's poetic genius and religious bent of mind would get little chance to escape the attentions of people in quest of spiritual values. From the age of twenty-six he became the central figure in Sikh affairs—and in a subtle way was far more powerful than the politicians and ministers who hit the headlines of newspapers every other day. This for two reasons. He was the man who brought about a renaissance of the Punjabi language after a virtual lapse of more than two centuries. Vir Singh also gave a fillip to the Sikh religion. Through his weekly journal, *Khalsa Samachar*, his books, *Guru Nanak Chamatkar, Kalgidhar Chamatkar* and many tracts which were given away in the millions, he told the story of the Sikh Gurus, their teachings and their achievements. His novels *Sundari, Bijai Singh* and *Satwant Kaur*, which make dull and didactic reading today, sold in the thousands because they gave the Sikhs of fifty years ago exactly what they wanted: an assurance of the excellence of their faith, a pride in the valour of their forefathers and a confidence in the traditions of orthodoxy handed down by the Gurus. Although Vir Singh was not the founder of the Singh Sabha movement which espoused these causes, he was more responsible for its achievements than all the other members put together.

LEARNING AND HUMILITY

Vir Singh's reaction to the adoration that came his way was that of a modest man with a deep-seated sense of humility. He was the one man who answered the Gita's definition of vidya vinaya sampanne—great humility which comes of great learning. As people clamoured to see him and hear him speak, he became less and less visible. He never appeared at public functions, he never made a speech, he never allowed anyone to photograph him. Not one of his many books carried his name on its jacket and he had written more than any Indian dead or alive: his complete works would be bulkier than the entire set of the *Encyclopaedia Britannica*. They represent over sixty years of uninterrupted writing of six to eight hours a day.

The sense of humility never left him and appears like a refrain in many of his verses. The achievement is never that of the human being but that of the Maker, who in his compassion, chose him to be his instrument of expression. Sometimes this sense becomes that of being used—or in the effeminate, masochistic extreme of being misused—for a divine purpose:

> Thou didst pluck and tear me from the branch
> Held me, breathed the fragrance
> And cast me away
> Thus discarded
> Trodden underfoot and mingled with the dust
> All I remember—and with gratitude—
> Is the memory of the touch.

The first time I saw him at a public meeting was at a kavi sammelan in Sargodha where he sat obscurely mixed up with the people. A young boy had recited a stirring ballad which had moved Vir Singh and he had asked to meet him. The news went around the 20,000-member audience that Vir Singh was among them; they clamoured for his darshan because all had read or heard of him, very few had seen him. He was almost dragged to the microphone on the platform. Roars of 'Sat Sri Akal' lasting a good fifteen minutes greeted him. All he could do was to fold his hands and mumble: 'Wahe Guruji ka Khalsa, Wahe Guruji ki Fateh.' Whichever way he turned thousands of heads bowed to touch the ground like a field of corn bending to the breeze. No Sikh since the Sikh Gurus could have known worship the way it was offered to Vir Singh; no one deserved it more.

NO CONVENTIONAL SAINT

Vir Singh did not look, live or behave like a conventional saint. He was not lean or ascetic in appearance; he was of medium height, of stocky build and with a long flowing beard. He dressed well and lived like an upper-class bourgeois person in a large house with a larger garden. He was married and had two daughters. He kept an excellent table. He was a strict vegetarian and a great stickler for cleanliness. All fruits and vegetables were regularly washed in potassium permanganate before they were cooked or consumed in his house. He had a great love for his garden and grew exotic strains of citrus—grapefruit and Malta oranges. His favourite flower was the narcissus, which blossomed in profusion in beds about his windows.

He was not indifferent to money; his poems fetched larger royalties than those of any other poet. Both he and his scholarly brother had a dominant voice in the affairs of a bank.

Vir Singh was hardly known outside the Sikh community ten years ago. It was only after the conferment of doctorates from universities, nomination to the Punjab Council, the Sahitya Akademi Award for 'Mere Sayan Jeo' and the Padma Bhushan that other people got to hear of him. That was not surprising, for although he was not narrow-minded in his outlook and had close associations with innumerable Hindus and a lifelong friendship with a Muslim doctor, Sikhs and the Sikh religion were his only preoccupation.

FAITH IN SIKHISM

The dominant impression that Vir Singh left on his visitors was one of gentleness. He spoke softly and what he said had the soothing quality of a salve. Here, again, was the mysterious something which he attributed to the Guru in his writing and possessed in good measure himself:

> As a cloud ambling along
> For a moment tarries
> To cast a cool shadow on the parched earth
> And send a welcome shower.

Vir Singh has gone but in his case it certainly is the casting off of worn-out clothes and donning new ones. Even while he lived, people knew him only through his writings which will live forever. Wherever the Punjabi language is spoken, there Vir Singh's name will be spoken too. And whenever the Sikhs begin to doubt their faith, there will be Vir Singh's spirit to inspire them and beckon them back to the fold.

DADAJI
(1909–1992)

I have no faith. I've never felt the need for it. Faith is denial of reason and for me reason is supreme. But I do not question the right of people to stick to their faiths because I have seen the good that it can do to some of them. I do not believe in miracles any more than I do in magic. But I do not deny that there are phenomena which still baffle scientists. I say this as a prelude to narrating my encounter with Amiya Roy Chowdhury, known to his innumerable admirers as Dadaji.

I received two books on Dadaji. They were compilations of tributes by eminent doctors, professors and businessmen, all of whom had experienced some miracle or the other. My interest was roused.

A few days later, film star Abhi Bhattacharya breezed into my office to take me to meet Dadaji. The happy glow on his handsome face made me suspect that he had already counted me among his dharma bhais.

I report the encounter without any prejudice or bias.

The reception room in Dadaji's apartment in Bandra had no furniture except a divan which was obviously meant for Dadaji. At the time there were only half a dozen men and women, all Bengalis. Then Dadaji entered. Everyone stood up. One man prostrated himself, placing his head on Dadaji's feet.

Dadaji is tall and light-skinned. He wears his black hair long. His youthful handsomeness belies his seventy years. His eyes have a hypnotic, spellbinding power. An aroma known in esoteric circles as the padmagandha (fragrance of the lotus) fills the room.

Dadaji seats himself on the divan and beckons to me. I shuffle up and sit near his feet. He tries to fix me in a kindly but hypnotic stare. He wants to know why I have come to see him. I tell him of my lack of faith, my disbelief in the existence of a divine power and my curiosity about him and his following.

'What if Sri Satya Narayan wants to communicate with you?'

he asks. I look puzzled. 'What if he sends you a memento?' he asks again. He raises his right hand in the air, and in his palm appears a medallion with an image of an elderly man. 'It is Sri Satya Narayan's gift to you,' assures Dadaji. 'No, it is not,' I protest. 'You, Dadaji, have given it to me.' He smiles. 'I am no one, it is all the doing of Sri Satya Narayan.

'What is your name?' he asks. I tell him. He takes back the medallion, rubs the reverse side with his thumb. What had been a blank surface is now embossed with my name. Only my name is not correctly spelt. A minute later, and as mysteriously as before, a gold chain appears in the palm of his empty hand. 'This is to wear the medallion around your neck,' he says, giving it to me.

'Come with me,' orders Dadaji. I follow him. He leads me into his bedroom.

Once more we are on different levels; he sits on his bed, I on the floor beside him. He tells me he is a monist. Sri Satya Narayan pervades the entire universe. There are no gurus. Each man is his own guru because he is a part of Sri Satya Narayan. The way to salvation is through Mahanam (the great name). It can be in any language.

'You ask for it in your own mother tongue.' He hands me a blank slip of paper and asks me to bow before a picture of Sri Satya Narayan. I do so. The paper now bears two words in Gurmukhi, 'Gopal, Govinda.' A minute later the paper is blank again. Apparently the message has been delivered and does not need to be on paper any more. And so it continues. A touch of his hand on my beard fills my beard with the same padmagandha.

For an unbeliever it is a traumatic kind of experience. It does not shake my disbelief in religion or miracles nor bends my reason to accept banal statements about God, Guru and the Name which pass for philosophy in our land. But let the reader make up his own mind.

WRITERS/ARTISTS

DHIREN BHAGAT
(1957–1988)

Two years ago Dhiren Bhagat wrote my obituary for an Indian journal. Some of it was flattering: my being larger than life and a journalist father-figure; some not so flattering: my undeserved and self-generated reputation of being a drunkard and a womanizer, whereas I had in fact slept with nothing more animated than a hot water bottle. Most of it was just having fun at my expense. Many people, who didn't read beyond the first few lines lamenting my demise, fired off long telegrams and letters of condolence to my 'widow'.

I live to write Dhiren Bhagat's obituary. He is, in fact, dead. It was an untimely death: he was only thirty-one. A cruel death: he was crushed under a bus while overtaking another. And a singularly tragic one as he was the only child of his parents and a young man with enormous promise as a writer and a journalist.

Dhiren came to see me soon after he returned from Oxford. He was a pretty, effeminate, red-lipped boy in gold-rimmed glasses, dressed in khadi kurta-pyjama with a silk shawl draped about his shoulders. He had the cultivated stutter of the English upper class. He had political aspirations and seemed to have acquired the neta's garb as the first step towards achieving netahood. I gathered he was related to my wife whose mother was a Bhagat. I got the impression that he was a phoney.

Then I began to see his articles in *The Spectator*. My opinion of him changed. They were extremely well-researched, witty, and beautifully worded. I became a fan. After reading some of his articles on Punjab, I persuaded him to do a book on the subject and took him to meet President Zail Singh. Thereafter, whenever he happened to be in Delhi he dropped in to see me. I took him out to dine with friends. Although a teetotaller and a vegetarian, he was great company. When it came to meeting deadlines, Dhiren proved to be elusive. He always had a plausible excuse: he was short of money and compelled to write for papers to meet his day-to-day expenses. My colleague in Penguin India, David Davidar, agreed with me that we should tie him down with a contract. He was the only author on our list to whom we paid an advance royalty.

Then he had another set of excuses: he had become a correspondent of *The Observer* (London); he was in love, jilted by his girlfriend and accident-prone: while covering the hola mohalla at Anandpur, he was knocked down by a cavalry of nihangs and badly bruised. He had to spend several days in hospital.

Every time we met he had some good reason for not submitting his manuscript. 'It is not going to be just a journalist's reportage but a work of art,' he would assure me. 'If you want your money back, I'll give you a cheque.' We decided to give him more time. Destiny did not. Penguin India is left poorer by a few thousand rupees; India has lost a man who might well have become one of its most illustrious sons.

R. K. NARAYAN
(1906–2001)

It must be over forty years ago that I first met R. K. Narayan in his hometown, Mysore. I had read some of his short stories and novels. I marvelled at how a storyteller of modern times could hold a reader's interest without injecting sex or violence into his narratives. I found them too slow-moving, without any sparkling sentences or memorable descriptions of nature or of his characters. Nevertheless, the one-horse town of his invention, Malgudi, had etched itself on my mind. And all my south Indian friends raved about him as the greatest of Indians writing in English. He certainly was among the pioneers comprising Raja Rao, Govind Desani and Mulk Raj Anand. Whether or not he was the best of them is a matter of opinion.

Being with Narayan on his afternoon strolls was an experience. He did not go to a park but preferred walking up to the bazaar. He walked very slowly and after every few steps he would halt abruptly to complete what he was saying. He would stop briefly at shops to exchange namaskaras with the owners, introduce me and exchange gossip with them in Kannada or Tamil, neither of which I understood. I could sense these gentle strolls in crowded bazaars gave him material for his novels and stories. I found him very likeable and extremely modest despite his achievements.

We saw a lot more of each other during a literary seminar organized by the East-West Centre in Hawaii. Having said our pieces and sat through discussions that followed, we went out for our evening walks, looking for a place to eat. It was the same kind of stroll that we had taken in Mysore, punctuated by abrupt halts in the middle of crowded pavements till he was ready to resume walking. Finding a suitable eatery posed quite a problem. Narayan was a strict teetotaller and a vegetarian; I was neither. We would stop at a grocery store where he bought himself a carton of yoghurt. Then we would go from one eatery to another with R. K. Narayan asking, 'Have you got boiled rice?' Eventually we would find one. Narayan would empty his carton of yoghurt on the mound of boiled rice. The only compromise he made was to eat it with a spoon instead of his fingers, which he would have preferred. Such eateries had very second-rate food and no wine. Dining out was no fun for me.

One evening I decided to shake off Narayan and have a ball on my own. 'I am going to see a blue movie. I don't think you will like it,' I told him. 'I'll come along with you, if you don't mind,' he replied. So we found ourselves in a sleazy suburb of Honolulu watching an extremely obscene film depicting all kinds of sexual deviations. I thought Narayan would walk out, or throw up. He sat stiffly without showing any emotion. It was I who said, 'Let's go.' He turned to me and asked kindly: 'Have you had enough?'

We should get Narayan in the proper perspective. He would not have gone very far but for the patronage of Graham Greene who also became a kind of literary agent for him. He also got the enthusiastic patronage of *The Hindu*. N. Ram and his former English wife, Susan, wrote an excellent biography of Narayan. Greene made Narayan known to the English world of letters; *The Hindu* made him a household name in India.

Narayan was a very lovable man, but his humility was deceptive. Once, when All India Radio invited a group of Indian writers to give talks and offered them fees far in excess of their usual rates, while all others accepted the offer, Narayan made it a condition that he should be paid at least one rupee more than the others. In his travelogue, *My Dateless Diary*, he writes about a dialogue at a luncheon party given in his honour. 'I blush to record this, but do it for documentary purposes. After the discussions [between two publishers declaring which of Narayan's novels is their favourite one, and ranking him with Hemingway and Faulkner as the world's three greatest living writers] have continued on these lines for a while, I feel I ought to assert my modesty—I interrupt them to say, "Thank you, but not yet…" They brush me aside and repeat, "Hemingway, Faulkner and Narayan, the three greatest living…"' Narayan goes on at some length about the argument between the publishers over whether to include Greene or Hemingway, besides Narayan himself, among the three greatest.

I was foolish enough to write about this in my column. Narayan never spoke to me again.

ALI SARDAR JAFRI
(1913–2000)

The day Ali Sardar Jafri died in Bombay on 1 August 2000, at 8.30 a.m., I made it a point to watch Pakistan Television to find out what it had to say about him. He was not only in the front-rank of Urdu poets of recent times but also the spearhead of the movement for a rapprochement with Pakistan. Pak TV made a passing reference to Jafri's death as a poet who wrote of the need for love and understanding between people. I was disappointed. So was I with the coverage given by the Indian media, both the print and the electronic. There was a lot more to Jafri than the hastily written obituaries and collages put together to meet deadlines.

I had known Ali Sardar and his beautiful wife, Sultana, for over thirty years. During my years in Bombay we met each other almost every other week. Despite his commitment to Communism, he liked the good things of life: good Scotch, good food and comfortable living. He lived in a pokey little three-room flat off Peddar Road. Apart from his wife and three children who often stayed with him, he had two widowed sisters in the same apartment. There was not much room to move about. Many of his books were stacked under his bed, on which he read, wrote and slept. I would arrive armed with a bottle of Scotch. He would send for soda and biryani from a restaurant, Allah Beli, facing his apartment. I sought his company because he was about the most erudite of Indian writers I had met.

Ali Sardar also had a phenomenal memory. If I quoted one line of any Urdu poet, he would come out with the rest of the poem. And explain every word by referring to Persian poets—from Rumi and Hafiz to Ghalib and Allama Iqbal. When I set about translating Iqbal's *Shikwa* and *Jawab-e-Shikwa*, I went all the way to Bombay to seek his assistance. For two days Ali Sardar and Sultana came to my hotel in the morning; we worked till lunchtime when Rafiq Zakaria and his wife Fatma joined us to find out how it was going. After they left, we resumed our labours till it was time for our sundowners.

I often needled Ali Sardar about his Communism. He had been a cardholder and had been expelled from the Aligarh Muslim University (which later gave him an honorary doctorate) and spent eighteen months in jail during the British Raj and again after Independence under Morarji Desai. Although he had ceased to be a cardholder, he stoutly defended Marxist ideology. What was beyond my comprehension was that despite professing atheism, during the month of Muharram he often wore black and attended Shia majlises and abstained from alcohol. During a TV interview with me, when he expected to be questioned about Urdu poetry, I confronted him with his contradictory beliefs in both Islam and Marxism. He was visibly upset and fumbled for words. He took it out on me after the interview was over. He called me everything under the sun short of calling me a bastard. I am sure if he had not been so obsessed with Communism and social problems, he would have made a great poet.

I saw him often when he came to Delhi to record the series *Kahkashaan* (Milky Way), on contemporary Urdu poets, and later to participate in the *Jashn-e-Bahaar* mushairas organized by Kamna to bring Pakistani and Urdu poets together on one stage every year. He presided over the last one a few months before he died.

He had an imposing presence: he was a lean, tall man with a mop of untidy, tousled grey hair, sparkling dark eyes and an ever-smiling face. His voice held his audience spellbound. His message to Pakistan at a time when Indo-Pak relations were at their worst was one of peace:

Tum aao gulshan-e-Lahore se chaman bardosh,
Hum aayen subh-e-Banaras ki roshnee le kar
Himalay ki havaaon ki taazgee le kar
Aur iske baad yeh poochein ki kaun dushman hai?

You come from the garden of Lahore laden with flowers,
We will come bearing the light of a Benaras morning
With fresh breezes from Himalayan heights
And then, together we can ask, who is the enemy?

Ali Sardar was an incorrigible optimist. Inspired by Rumi's line, Hum cho sabza baarha roeeda aym (like the green of the earth we never stop growing), he summed up his life story (Mera Safar) in a few memorable lines:

> I am a fleeting moment
> In the magic house of days and nights;
> I am a restless drop travelling eternally
> From the flask of the past to the goblet of the future.
> I sleep and wake, awaken to sleep again;
> I am the ancient play on the stage of time
> I die only to become immortal.

Ali Sardar, who was born into a zamindar family in Balrampur, Uttar Pradesh, on 29 November 1913, won numerous awards for his poems, short stories, plays and articles. They included the Iqbal Samman, Soviet Land Nehru Award, Sant Jnaneshwar Award and the Jnanpith Award. More than all those it was the warm-hearted applause he won wherever he went, the respect and affection he received from people he knew that sustained him during his difficult days. He returned the love he got in full measure. In a collection of his poems he gave to Kamna Prasad's four-year-old daughter Jia, he wrote the word pyaar in Urdu five times on each line down twenty lines. That was his parting message to the world.

FIRAQ GORAKHPURI
(1896–1982)

There is a gross misconception that Urdu is the language of Muslims. There were, and are today, many good poets of Urdu who are Hindus. The greatest among them was Raghupati Sahai, better known as Firaq Gorakhpuri. He was a Kayastha from Gorakhpur, Uttar Pradesh. Besides being a good poet, he had a good academic record and qualified for the civil services. He resigned to join the freedom movement and spent some months in jail with Jawaharlal Nehru.

For four years he was the undersecretary of the Congress. He topped in the MA examinations, taught English at Allahabad University before retiring as reader in 1958. In 1961, he won the Sahitya Akademi Award, two years later the Soviet Land Nehru Award and in 1970 the Jnanpith Award. He wrote in Hindi, Urdu and English but opted for Urdu as the better medium to put across his ideas. He soon came to be sought after for mushairas. His closest rival and friend was an equally good poet—the Muslim Josh Malihabadi.

Besides the love of poetry, they shared much in common. Both were patriotic, loved the good things in life, were connoisseurs of liquor and women. Many bawdy stories were told about them. Both thought immensely of their looks and talents and boasted about their prowess as poets and lovers. Firaq had a disastrous marriage and wrote a lot of nasty things about the woman who bore him two children. (Their daughter died young, their son committed suicide.)

Firaq admitted that often it took him weeks to perfect a couple of lines of poetry. He was one Urdu poet who, instead of turning to Arabic and Persian vocabulary and imagery, as most poets of the language did, injected a lot of Hindi words into his poems. Instead of using Laila Majnu, the bulbul, the rose, the moth and flame as symbols of eternal love, he turned to Radha and Krishna. He also used a lot of the imagery from Keats, Shelley, Wordsworth and Tennyson in his compositions. Firaq's ideal of a female companion was:

Moan our behen bhi, our chehetee bhi
Ghar ki rani bhi aur jeewan sathi
Phir bhi voh kamini sarasar devi
Aur seyj par voh heswa ki petlee.

Mother, sister and a daughter I adore
Queen of my home, life companion and more
Also much desired as a goddess as well
But when in bed a voluptuous whore.

When Malihabadi decided to migrate to Pakistan because he could not find suitable husbands for his daughters in India, Firaq was deprived of a friend and a rival with whom he could cross swords. When he heard of Malihabadi's death, he is supposed to have said, 'Once again the fellow has beaten me to it.' He died a few days later.

NIRAD C. CHAUDHURI
(1897–1999)

'There is nothing more dreadful to an author than neglect, compared with which reproach, hatred and opposition are names of happiness.' These words of Dr Samuel Johnson were inscribed by Nirad Chaudhuri in my copy of his book *A Passage to England*. These words hold the key to Nirad's past life and present personality. They explain the years of neglect of one who must have, at all times, been a most remarkable man; his attempts to attract attention by cocking a snook at people who had neglected him; and the 'reproach, hatred and opposition' that he succeeded in arousing as a result of his rudeness.

Nirad had been writing in Bengali for many years. But it was not until the publication of his first book in English, *The Autobiography of an Unknown Indian*, that he really aroused the interest of the class to which he belonged and which, because of the years of indifference to him, he had come heartily to loathe—the anglicized upper-middle class of India. He did this with calculated contempt. He knew that the wogs were more English than Indian but were fond of proclaiming their patriotism at the expense of the British. That having lost their own traditions and not having fully imbibed those of England, they were a breed with pretensions to intellectualism that seldom went beyond reading blurbs and reviews of books.

He therefore decided to dedicate the work 'To the British Empire...' The wogs took the bait and, having read only the dedication, sent up a howl of protest. Many people who would not have otherwise read the autobiography, discovered to their surprise that there was nothing anti-Indian in its pages. On the contrary, it was the most beautiful picture of eastern Bengal that anyone had ever painted. And at long last, India had produced a writer who did not cash in on naive Indianisms but could write the English language as it should be written—and as few, if any, living Englishmen could write.

Nobody could afford to ignore Nirad Chaudhuri any more. He and his wife Amiya became the most sought-after couple in Delhi's upper-class circles. Anecdotes of his vast fund of knowledge were favourite topics at dinner parties.

The first story I heard of the Chaudhuri family was of a cocktail party given by the late Director General of All India Radio, Colonel Lakshmanan. Nirad had brought his wife and sons (in shorts and full boots) to the function. After the introductions, the host asked what Nirad would like to drink: he had some excellent sherry.

'What kind of sherry?' asked the chief guest. Colonel Lakshmanan had, like most people, heard of only two kinds. 'Both kinds,' he replied. 'Do you like dry or sweet?' This wasn't good enough for Nirad, so he asked one of his sons to taste it and tell him. The thirteen-year-old lad took a sip, rolled it about his tongue and after a thoughtful pause replied, 'Must be an Oloroso 1947.'

Nirad Babu could talk about any subject under the sun. There was not a bird, tree, butterfly or insect whose name he did not know in Latin, Sanskrit, Hindi and Bengali. Long before he left for London, he not only knew where the important monuments and museums were, but also the location of many famous restaurants. I heard him contradict a lady who had lived six years in Rome about the name of a street leading off from the Colosseum—and prove his contention. I've heard him discuss stars with astronomers, recite lines from an obscure fifteenth-century French poet to a professor of French literature, advise a wine dealer on the best vintages from Burgundy. At a small function in honour of Halldór Laxness, the Icelandic winner of the Nobel Prize in Literature, I heard Nirad lecture him on Icelandic literature.

Nirad was a small, frail man, a little over five feet tall. He led a double life. At home he dressed in dhoti-kurta and sat on the floor to do his reading and writing. When leaving for office, he wore European dress: coat, tie, trousers and a monstrous khaki sola topi. As soon as he stepped out street urchins would chant 'Johnnie Walker, left, right, left, right'.

Nirad Babu was not a modest man; he had much to be immodest about. He was also a very angry man. He had much to be angry about. When he was dismissed from service by a singularly half-baked Minister of I & B, Dr B. V. Keskar, he exploded with wrath. But the combination of pride and anger has made life somewhat difficult for him and his family. Success has not mellowed him.

The Autobiography, despite its greatness as a work of art, was not a bestseller. With the job gone and three growing sons on his hands, life became hard for the Chaudhuri family. Many jobs were open to him; commissions for articles and broadcasts (from foreign countries) could have come to him for the asking, but what Nirad has never done is sell himself for money.

An incident illustrates the man's unending adherence to his principles. Some years after his dismissal, the then finance minister, T. T. Krishnamachari, summoned me to his office and asked me to persuade Nirad to write a series of articles on the plight of the Bengal refugees on any terms he liked. I told the minister of the official ban on Nirad. Armed with the assurance that it would be raised, I asked Nirad over to break the good news to him personally. When he came, I told him of the enthusiasm with which Krishnamachari (and H. M. Patel) had referred to his writing and how they were willing to give him a blank cheque and clear official objections.

He sat back in the chair for a couple of minutes without saying a word and then asked me in a slow, gentle voice, 'So the Government of India has decided to raise its ban on me?'

'Yes, it has.'

'But I haven't decided to raise my ban on the Government of India.' Without another word, he picked up his sola topi and walked out of the office.

Chaudhuri's second book, *A Passage to England*, received the most glorious reviews in the English press. Three editions were rapidly sold out and it had the distinction of becoming the first book by an Indian author to have become a bestseller in England. The bay windows of London's famous bookshop, Foyles, were decorated with large-sized photographs of Nirad. Some Indian critics were, as in the past, extremely hostile. Nirad's reaction followed the same pattern. At first he tried not to be bothered by people 'who didn't know better', then burst out with invective against the 'yapping curs'. I asked him how he reconciled himself to these two attitudes. After a pause he replied, 'When people say nasty things about my books without really understanding what I have written, I feel like a father who sees a drunkard make an obscene pass at his daughter. I want to chastise him.' Then, with a typically Bengali gesture demonstrating the form of chastisement, 'I want to give them a shoe-beating with my chappal.'

A few years ago, Nirad Babu wrote an article for a prestigious London weekly in which he mentioned how hard he was finding life in Oxford, living on his royalties from books. I published extracts from it in my column. K. K. Birla wrote to me to tell Nirad Babu that he would be happy to give him a stipend for life for any amount in any currency he wanted. I forwarded Birla's letter to Nirad. He wrote back asking me to thank Birla for his generous offer but refused to accept it. It is a pity that he accepted a CBE (Commander of the British Empire) from the British government. He deserved a peerage because he was in fact a peerless man of intellect and letters.

MULK RAJ ANAND
(1905–2004)

Way back in the 1940s, a few friends with literary ambitions formed a circle which met once a week to read poems and stories we had written. It was a mutual admiration society where glasses of whisky were refilled at the end of each recitation. We heard of Indian writers Mulk Raj Anand and R. K. Narayan making good in England with the publication of their novels. Eagerly we laid our hands on their books and discussed them in our meetings. We were a conceited lot and generally agreed that if Mulk and Narayan could find publishers abroad, so could we. When Mulk visited Punjab after making a name for himself in England, he was acclaimed as a pioneer of Indo-Anglian writing. He agreed to come to one of our meetings. He expected to be lionized; he was visibly put off with the cool reception he got. 'You chaps don't know what it takes to write a novel,' he snapped, 'talk to me after you have had one accepted by a publisher.' He had every right to snub us.

My view of Mulk and Narayan has not changed over the years. Both were indeed pioneers of Indo-Anglian fiction in their own way, prolific in their output but mediocre craftsmen.

Mulk's novels were propaganda stuff with a sheen of fiction: *Untouchable, Coolie, Two Leaves and a Bud*. They were designed to rouse the conscience of readers to the indignities inflicted by the well-to-do on the poor and make Britishers feel guilty about their racist colonialism. He was duly lauded by British Liberals and Leftists. Narayan was content to remain a storyteller, combining simple themes about people living at a leisurely pace in an imaginary small town—Malgudi. He was more widely acclaimed than Mulk, particularly in South India.

But both had one thing in common—they were both pioneers.

Mulk was born in Peshawar (12 December 1905) but spent his formative years in school and college in Amritsar. He often described himself as an Umbersaria. He was of short stature with a mop of curly hair and a pouting lower lip. He was never at a loss for words and could hold forth by the hour, often waffling thuth, thuth, when he was worked up. Even when addressing a meeting where every speaker was given five to ten minutes to speak, Mulk would go on rambling for half an hour, taking no notice of the bell to tell him his time was over, nor a tap on his shoulder. He often dwelt at length on how his father often beat his mother, and what effect it had on him as a child. He never forgave his father and was diagnosed by no less a psychoanalyst than Dr Sigmund Freud as suffering from acute mother fixation.

Mulk was very proud of being an Indian, of India's great legacy of art, sculpture, painting, its style of architecture (havelis), its way of living and etiquette. Once at a ghazal concert in London, he sat in the first row and applauded at the end of every couplet and was acknowledged by a polite salaam.

No one else in the audience knew it was the polite thing to do. An English friend I had taken with me asked me in a whisper, 'Who is that little fellow barking "Wow! Wow!" while the fellow is singing?' I told him who Mulk was and that he was not barking but saying 'Wah! Wah! Wonderful! Wonderful!', which was the done thing.

Although Mulk spent some time with Gandhiji in his ashram, he was much closer to the Communist Party in his politics. He was closely affiliated to the Progressive Writers' Association and the People's Theatre Group. This made him anathema to right-wingers. Once he was foolish enough to become an easy target for them. He was invited by *Evergreen Review* of New York to write a long article on the erotic in Indian art. A week after the article appeared, profusely illustrated with pictures of sculptures from Khajuraho and paintings from *Kamasutra*, the magazine received a legal notice from a Prof. Campbell of Sarah Lawrence College of New York alleging the article had been lifted from his translation from German on the same subject. Poor Mulk was asked to elucidate. He took great pains to exonerate himself. This was good enough for communist-baiter Dosu Karaka, editor of *Current*, to splash the news on the front page of his weekly tabloid with the banner headline 'Commie writer caught plagiarizing'. It took many months for Mulk to be able to appear in public.

I visited Mulk a couple of times in his ground floor flat on Cuffe Parade in Mumbai. He had a specially designed high chair with a slab in front to place his papers to write. It looked very much like a baby's chair put alongside a dining table. Mulk sat on it, resting his feet on the rung below, and scribbled away by the hour.

Though no Casanova, women of different nationalities were drawn to him like moths to a flame. He was a celebrity and they enjoyed being seen with him. He married more than twice and had several lady friends. His one child through an English wife coauthored a most readable biography of Maharaja Dalip Singh.

Mulk's lasting legacy is *Marg*, a magazine devoted to the arts financed by the Tatas. It had, and has, a limited circulation but is unique, being the only one on the subject and of high quality. He received many awards including one from the Sahitya Akademi and a Padma Bhushan. His word counted a great deal in official circles, particularly among senior babus who knew no more than the titles of his books, but were awed by his reputation. He was able to persuade them to make grants for writers' homes in Delhi and Lonavala. Usually he was the sole occupant of these homes.

What I have written may not sound like a tribute to a celebrated author. For this I crave pardon from Mulk's millions of admirers. But when I heard of his death in Pune, on 28 September 2004, at the age of ninety-nine, I was overcome with grief. I may not have held him in great esteem as a writer, but I recall him with great affection.

QURRATULAIN HYDER
(1927–2007)

Ask anyone who is knowledgeable about Urdu literature who he or she thinks was the best writer of fiction in the language, chances are that nine out of ten will reply: Qurratulain Hyder. If you probe them further on what they think her best work was, without hesitation they will answer: *Aag ka Darya (River of Fire)*. The novel earned her the Sahitya Akademi Award and the Jnanpith Award. It is, deservedly, described as something of a trailblazer in Urdu fiction.

Qurratulain Hyder, or Annie Apa as she was known to her friends, was about the most erudite woman around. She wore her erudition on her sleeve and offloaded it in large dollops in her novels and short stories with didactic zeal. While regaling her readers with episodes from the past and the present, she wanted to educate them on subjects like history, geography, religion (Buddhism, Jainism, Hinduism, Islam), mysticism (both Sufi and Bhakti), rituals, Eastern and Western classical music as well as modern pop, poetry (Hindi, Urdu, English), flora and fauna. There was nothing in the world that Aunty Annie did not know and she wanted to make sure that her readers were impressed with her vast fund of knowledge. Most were.

River of Fire was Annie at her best. She spreads a vast canvas to paint on. She starts with Chandragupta and his minister Chanakya, deals with the conflicts between the established Buddhist religion and resurgent Hinduism, the advent of Islam, establishment of Muslim dynasties, arrival of European traders, dominance of the East India Company, English nabobs with harems of Indian bibis and their Eurasian offspring, the consolidation of British rule, upsurge of Indian nationalism, the Mutiny of 1857, the First and Second World Wars, the Congress Party, the Muslim League, the Partition of India and Pakistan, the post-Independence era up to 1956. It leaves the reader breathless. Hundreds of characters come and vanish from the scene. What stays in the reader's mind are Hindu and Muslim families of Lucknow,

Jaunpur, Moradabad and Varanasi, bound by similar backgrounds and bonds of affection. 'In Lucknow history is yesterday,' asserts the author. It overtakes them and splits them apart. Some flee to England, some to Pakistan, some stay on in India where they cannot come to terms with the changed atmosphere; they cry in anguish, 'Why did you forsake me, India!'

A melancholic strain of nostalgia for the days gone by runs like a refrain throughout the novel. It is aptly summed up by Toru Dutt's lines:

> O echo whose repose I mar
> With my regrets and mournful cries
> He comes...
> I hear his voice afar,
> Or is it thine that thus replied?
> Peace: hark he calls!—in vain, in vain.
> The loved and lost, comes not again.

River of Fire could have been the most powerful historical novel of India but for some minor, avoidable flaws. There are far too many passages which sound like so many words devoid of meaning. To wit:

> The picture of the world was merely the Self which had been painted on the canvas of the Self. This was that pure existence, pure perception, pure life, the studio of the heart which contained all pictures, all imagination, where all images became one, where the same light kept passing through myriad-coloured glasses and all that which had been made with beauty and truth was a complete art-piece and a path, both for the creator and the beholder. And those who knew could understand.

This may be overlooked as expounding some abstruse aspect of Buddhist philosophy, but Hyder's penchant for depicting scenes was far too often stereotyped. She was not as close to nature as she set herself out to be. Her dhak (flame of the forest) flowers in Bhadon (the season of rains) when in fact it flowers for a few days around Holi. She put the battlefield of Plassey in a mango orchard; it was in a forest of palas (another name for flame of the forest). Her fair maidens sporting by river banks have magnolia petals dropping on their heads; there are very few magnolias in India and, unlike American and European trees of the species, have very sparse blossoms. Her hill partridges 'coo'; in fact, hill partridges make calls that grate on the ears.

Hyder insisted on translating her works into English herself: she was convinced she knew it as well as Urdu. So we have thees, thous along with yeah, yep, omigosh and get lost. But no one dared tell Annie Apa that she should allow someone else to handle her fiction. She was the subjantiwali. If *River of Fire* did not become the rage in English that it was in Urdu, she had only herself to blame.

NIRALA
(1896–1961)

Even those who don't read Hindi know the poet Nirala (rare) as a highly eccentric character, a *moonh phat* (face-spitter) who took on Bapu Gandhi and Jawaharlal Nehru, had a crush on Vijaylakshmi Pandit (it was never reciprocated) and went crackers in the last years of his life. Now, for the first time, I have been able to read his work translated into English—*A Season on the Earth: Selected poems of Nirala*. It has been translated by David Rubin, once professor of Hindi at Columbia University. I have come to the conclusion that besides being a crackpot, Nirala was a great poet, and Rubin is a great translator.

Suryakant Tripathi was born in 1896 in the village Mahishadal (district Midnapur, West Bengal), in a family of Kanyakubja Brahmins who had migrated from Kanauj (Uttar Pradesh). He spoke both Hindi and Bengali fluently. He took on the poetic pseudonym Nirala in 1923. He lost his mother when he was only two years old. Nirala married Manohradevi (then eleven) from Kanauj. He failed in his matriculation examination and was thrown out of his home by his father. He lived for many years with his wife's parents, and a son and a daughter were born to him. Despite early setbacks, Nirala made his name as a poet.

He went to Calcutta to edit a magazine for the Ramakrishna Mission and then another journal, *Matvala*. He then moved to Lucknow where he lived for twelve years and saw the publication of his collection of poems, *Anamika*. He came to be known as the 'Tagore of Hindi'. Gandhi made the mistake of asking his hosts at a meeting of Hindi litterateurs in Indore in 1936: 'Where is the Tagore of Hindi?' Sometime later, Gandhi happened to be in Lucknow. When Nirala went to see him, Gandhi's secretaries stopped him saying he was seeing some important politicians. Nirala snapped back: 'I am an even more important poet.'

Another time he cornered Nehru in a rail compartment and demanded to know why he had failed to pay tribute to Munshi

Premchand on his death. In his later years Nirala began to have illusions of grandeur. He claimed to be a wealthy man, attached university degrees to his name and talked of his dialogues with Queen Victoria. He coined his own obituary a long time before he died. When visitors came to call on him, he would tell them, 'Nirala doesn't live here. The man you are looking for died long ago.' He died in a mental home in 1961.

Nirala was a poet of rare sensibility towards nature and feminine beauty. In an early composition he describes a young girl:

> She sat on a rock,
> Her blue skirt gently fluttering—thus,
> Uninhibited, the evening breeze
> Held some silent conversation with the lovely girl
> And smiled.
> Her curling hair,
> Black and luxuriant,
> Blue, loose and fragrant over her pale face,
> Tumbled over her breasts,
> Teased her affectionately.
> From the open sky
> The chill spray scattered,
> Exhilarating,
> On her shapely limbs.

In an earlier poem composed in 1916, which roused some controversy, he compared the blossoming of a jasmine bud to that of a young girl being embraced by her lover:

> On a vine in the deserted wood
> She slept, blissful in dreams of love,
> Pure tender slender girl—
> The juhi bud—
> Eyes closed, languorous in the folded leaf.
> A spring night. Her lover,
> Tormented by separation in a distant land,
> Was that wind they call

The southern sandal-mountain breeze.
He recalled their sweet reunions,
The midnight drenched in moonlight,
The lovely trembling body of the girl.
And then? That wind
Crossed over grove lake river mountain wood
And vine-entangled jungles
To reach where he could dally with the
budding flower.
She slept—
For, tell me, how could she suspect
That her lover was at her side?
The hero kissed her cheek,
And she swayed, shivering from it,
But even now she did not waken
Nor ask forgiveness for her fault.
The long curved sleepy eyes stayed shut
As though she swooned,
Intoxicated from the wine of youthful
longings—who can say? Ruthless, her lover,
Of a sudden cruel,
Struck that tender body hard,
Slapped her pale full cheeks.
The girl started up,
Stared all about her, astonished,
And found her darling by her bed.
She smiled, gratified in her desire,
And blossomed in her lover's arms.

GHALIB
(1797–1869)

If you want to know what the greatest figure in Urdu literature, Mirza Asadullah Khan Ghalib, looked like and how he lived in the Delhi of his times, you will not find it in his poetry, which is often difficult to comprehend. You will, however, find it in the letters he wrote to his friends and admirers. An inveterate letter-writer, he wrote four to five letters a day and even posted them himself. Most of his correspondents were aspiring poets who sent him their compositions to correct; he did so with great care. In his replies, he invariably put in a couplet or two of his own and gave a detailed account of how he was faring.

Asadullah Khan was a handsome man—tall, light-skinned and with an imperious martial bearing. His forefathers, Seljuk Turks, were professional soldiers. Asad was a man of peace and, even as a boy, liked to study Arabic, Persian and Urdu. He was convinced that he was not going to be a soldier but a poet. He took on the pseudonym Ghalib. He was married off in his teens. His wife bore him seven sons and daughters, all of whom died in their infancy. He moved to Delhi to gain access to Mughal King Bahadur Shah Zafar, a poet of substance, and the nobility which patronized poets. His wife proved to be a poor companion. For companionship and pleasure, Ghalib sought the company of dancing girls and prostitutes. He never earned enough to maintain his household in comfort and was always in debt to moneylenders.

When the Sepoy Mutiny broke out in 1857, Ghalib had no sympathy with the mutineers and stopped calling on King Bahadur Shah Zafar, who had become a puppet in their hands. During the months the fighting lasted, he did not go out of his house. Evidently, families of Muslim hakims, who lived in Ballimaran, which was where Ghalib had his residence, also did not support the mutineers. Consequently, when the British and their Indian allies re-occupied Delhi, they drove out Muslims whom they suspected of supporting the mutineers but allowed Ballimaran Muslims to stay on. Raja Mohinder Singh of Patiala put his troops at both ends of the bazaar to ensure their safety.

Ghalib mentions his daily routine in many letters to his friends and patrons. He was not an early riser because his nights were disturbed by the malfunctioning of his bladder; he had to get up to urinate every hour. He had a frugal breakfast of peeled almonds and syrups; mutton broth at midday; and four kababs and an ounce of wine mixed with rose water made up his dinner. During the mango season, he consumed up to twelve mangoes in one sitting every afternoon. His bowels were often out of order and boils would erupt all over his body. He was full of remorse: 'I am old, idiotic, sinful, sensual, profligate and, withal, a man lost to shame.' He describes himself as 'sattra-bahattra'. Before he was seventy, he started losing his memory, vision and hearing.

Ghalib did not take religious injunctions too seriously. He had his own version of Roza during Ramadan. He wrote: 'I observe fasts, but keep my fasts well-humoured with occasional sips of water, and a few puffs of the hookah. Now and then I eat a few morsels of bread also. People here have a strange sense of things and a strange disposition. I am just whiling away the fast, but they accuse me of non-observance of this holy ritual. They should understand that skipping the fasts is one thing, and whiling them away is quite another.'

He never spared himself from self-criticism. 'I have learned to enjoy even my griefs and insults. I imagine myself as a different entity, separate from myself. When a fresh misfortune befalls me, I say, "Well served. Ghalib receives another slap in his face. How proud he was. How he used to brag that he was a great poet and a Persian scholar without peer far and near. Well, deal with the moneylenders now.

"But how can this shameless fellow speak? He borrowed money left and right—wine from the cellar, flowers from the florist, clothes from the draper, mangoes from the fruit seller, and money from the creditors. He should have realized that he had no means to repay the debts."'

He had occasional outbursts of temper. When his publisher inserted some other poets' lines in his collection, he exploded: 'I do not know the b.....d who has inserted into my diwan the verses that you have sent me. May this scoundrel, his father, his grandfather, and his great-grandfather, right back to his seven adulterous generations, be damned.'

Ghalib also knew his worth. When somebody asked him for his postal address, he cut him down to size: 'Asadullah Ghalib, Delhi, will be enough.' So it was. And is today. Delhi is known as the city where Ghalib lived and died.

MIR TAQI MIR
(1725–1810)

Did you know that at one time Urdu novelists and chroniclers used to have appendices to their works in which they included their favourite jokes which had nothing whatsoever to do with the themes of their books? I discovered this after reading Mir Taqi Mir's autobiography, *Zikr-i-Mir*, translated from Persian into English by C. M. Naim, professor of Urdu at Chicago University. In my list of the great masters of Urdu, the name of Mir Taqi Mir would be among the top five. My interest in him was not as a poet of great merit but as a chronicler of the times in which he lived. While working on *Delhi: A Novel*, which I based largely on eyewitness accounts, I was looking for someone who had seen and written of the devastation caused to Delhi by two invaders, the Persian, Nadir Shah, and the Afghan, Ahmed Shah Abdali. I found Mir Taqi Mir. He was born in Agra, spent most of his life in Delhi and its neighbourhood, and when the situation became intolerable, migrated to Lucknow where he died. Mir wrote his autobiography in Persian. Since I do not know Persian, I had to rely on its Urdu translation. He did not write very much about himself, his love affairs, his wife or children, but largely about his father, his friends, his patrons and fellow poets. I made up personal details of his life from my imagination and created a few scenes with the help of his poems which I translated. I knew my readers would forgive me for the liberties I took because my version was a mixture of fact and fiction. I was eager to find an authentic biography of Mir and was delighted when I found *Zikr-i-Mir*.

Mir Taqi Mir lived through turbulent times as the Mughal empire began to disintegrate after the death of Emperor Aurangzeb (1707). The Persian invader, Nadir Shah, dealt it a near-death blow in 1738. He was followed by the Afghan, Ahmed Shah Abdali, who invaded India nine times and laid waste the whole of northern India. The Marathas, Jats, Rohilas, Pathans and Sikhs did their share of pillaging and looting. Mir gives vivid descriptions of the havoc caused by these unruly elements. He was particularly harsh in his judgement of the Sikhs. He wrote:

> The arrogance of these people (the Afghans) had crossed all limits; and so God, in his justice, decided to humiliate them at the hands of the Sikhs—men of no consequence, highway robbers, peasants, lowly men of no means, name or place; mean, destitute and disreputable people of that area. Some forty or fifty thousand of them came together and challenged that mighty army. Sometimes they boldly attacked and fought, and did not run away despite getting severely mauled. Other times, they attacked them, withdrew in different directions, pursued by small bodies of (Afghan) soldiers, whom they later slaughtered. Every morning they created some new mischief, and each evening they attacked from every side. They sent the soldiers of the Shah scurrying every which way, desperately trying to make an escape. Sometimes they suddenly appeared and pounced upon the baggage train and the people who followed the army. Other times they came in large numbers, and resolutely attacking some town, turned it into ruins. With tangled hair or a piece of cloth wrapped around their heads, they penetrated the camp itself. There was noise and tumult all night long, and all day long there was a hue and cry. Their foot soldiers attacked the Shah's horsemen with swords and filled their saddles with blood; and their retainers pounced upon the Shah's archers and tortured them to death. In short, these unworthy wretches (be-namusan-be-daulat) humiliated those vain-glorious brutes (be-hagigatan-be-muravaat) to such an extent that the chief of the region, on hearing of what had been happening, also stopped showing the Afghans any respect.

Mir Taqi Mir had a keen eye for detail. Having led a life of near starvation for most of his years, he was most impressed by a feast laid out by the nawab of Awadh for the British Governor General. He writes:

As for the types of breads at meal times: nan-i-badam (almond bread) of utmost delicacy; shirmal and bagar-khani, both coloured with saffron on the top that would put the sun to shame; nan-i-javan (youthful bread), so soft and warm that if an old man were to eat it he would act like a youth, nan-i-varaqi (paper bread) of such a quality that I could fill a whole book with its praise, nan-i-zanjabi (ginger bread), so flavourful that taste itself grows happy thinking of it. In the middle were placed varieties of qaliya and do-piyaza, such rich stews of different kinds that the guests were all delighted and satisfied. And the kababs that were laid out on the long table-cloth; kabab-i-gul (flower kabab), full of bloom and flavour, perfectly salted kabab-i-hindi (Indian kabab) stole every heart; kabab-i-gandhari attracted all and sundry to itself; kabab-i-sang (stone kabab) brought relief to those who were tired from the hardships of the journey; kabab-i-varaq (paper kakab) was of such an amazing recipe that it delighted everyone; and all the more common kababs, spicy and flavourful. Ten large plates of food were placed before every single guest. Then there were pulaos of all kinds and wonderful soups of every type. 'Praise be to the One who is Bountiful and Generous!'

I was not impressed by Mir's sense of humour. Many of the anecdotes quoted by Professor Naim are outrageously ribald and would not be acceptable to editors of today. A borderline joke goes as follows: 'Two men were close friends; they were also engaged, each to the other's sister. By chance the astrologers also set the same date and time for the two weddings. Mulla Muhammad Baqir Majlisi was invited to perform the weddings but, due to another obligation, he excused himself. Instead he sent his nephew, Mulla Muhammad Ashraf, who had a jocular bent of mind. Ashraf came and performed the weddings. Then he turned to the two grooms, and said, "Why are you still sitting here? Go and start poking into each other's sisters." A repartee I found acceptable runs as follows: 'Once, in the Pavilion of Pleasure, the Shah asked Mirza Sahib to have some wine. When the Mirza declined, the Shah asked for a reason. 'It takes away one's intelligence,' the Mirza replied. The Shah didn't accept that and pressed him even more. Finally, the

Mirza gave in, and became so drunk that, by midnight, he had to be removed from the gathering. The next morning, when he again came to the court, the Shah said to him, "You made quite a mess of yourself last night. No one should be so shallow when it comes to holding his liquor." The Mirza said, "I humbly told you that wine takes away one's intelligence." The Shah retorted, "But then didn't I drink too?"

"May I die for you, sir," the Mirza replied, "but the reasoning concerned losing one's intelligence—you had none to begin with.'"

DOM MORAES
(1938–2004)

Dom Moraes's interest in poetry was born very early in his life. In his preface to a collection of his poems, he wrote, 'I was about ten years old when I started to read poetry... I had an instinctive feel, even at that age, for the shape and texture of words.' By the time he was fourteen, Dom—Domsky to his friends—had begun to write poetry himself, and he learned French in order to be able to read François Villon in the original. Poetry became a lifelong passion and he continued to write till the end of his life.

Dom was my friend from his years at Jesus College, Oxford. He was a complex character who disliked everything about India, particularly Indians—the only exceptions he made were the good-looking women he took to bed. Although he was born in Bombay, and was dark as a Goan, Dom considered himself English, spoke no Indian language and wished to be buried in the churchyard of Odcombe, a tiny village in Somerset. Never a practicing Christian, he selected Odcombe because one Thomas Coryate, who hailed from the village, had travelled all the way from England to India in the seventeenth century and died in Surat, where he is buried—and Dom went to Odcombe with Sarayu Srivatsa, his companion during the last decade and a half of his life, to collect material on Coryate's background for his biography. Despite his distaste for India, however, Dom's descriptions of the Indian countryside—of the heat and dust storms of summer, of the monsoons—were lyrically beautiful. His characters too came alive in his writing; notwithstanding his ignorance of Indian languages, Dom was able to comprehend what people said in their dialects and in Indian English.

Like his father, Frank Moraes, Dom was a heavy drinker. Because of his love for the bottle, Dom could not be depended on to meet deadlines or stick to the subject he was commissioned to write on. Ramnath Goenka of the *Indian Express* sacked Dom for spending his time in a Calcutta hotel, drinking and consorting with a lady instead of going on his assignment to the Northeast. His friend R. V. Pandit fired him for drinking in his office in Hong Kong. The *Times of India* appointed him editor of a magazine they intended to bring out, but they fired him before the first issue came out; Dom vented his anger on poor Prem Shankar Jha, who was appointed in his stead, by grabbing his tie and demanding: 'Fatty boy! What do you know about journalism?'

I had got Dom an assignment from the Dempos, shipping magnates and mine-owners of Goa; Dom produced a very readable book on Goa without mentioning the Dempos—I had to add four pages on the family. He was commissioned by the Madhya Pradesh tourism department to do a book on the state's historical sites; he did a creditable job of describing the beauty of the landscape and the state's full-bosomed tribal women, without bothering about historical sites. Dom never allowed facts or truths to stand in the way of his writing. He did not write reference books; instead, he painted pictures in vivid colours to the songs of flutes.

Dom is said to have married thrice. When he was married to the actress Leela Naidu (his third wife), I stayed with them in Hong Kong; they, in turn, visited me several times in Delhi. At the best of times, Dom spoke in a low mumble, hard to understand—when I had asked Indira Gandhi, whom he interviewed many times to write her biography, if she understood what he said, she had beamed and replied, 'No, Leela Naidu translated for me.' Dom's second wife, Judy, bore him a son, although I don't think Dom paid for his education; neither am I sure if he had church or civil weddings and court divorces. In any event, he certainly did not pay any alimony to his former wives—he never earned enough to do so.

Dom was not choosy about his women: if any of them were willing, he was always ready to oblige. The only real love of his life, I think, was Sarayu, a Tamil Brahmin married to a Punjabi and the mother of two children.

Sarayu was instrumental in helping Dom overcome the writers' block that plagued him for seventeen long years, from 1965 to 1982. In partnership with her, Dom wrote *Out of God's Oven*, perhaps the most fascinating example of his condemnation of all things Indian that he hated. Between them, Dom and Sarayu traversed the length and breadth of India, interviewing poets, writers, editors, film producers, Naxalites, Ranbir Sena leaders, dacoits and politicians—and Dom decried the resurgence of Hindu fundamentalism in the Bajrang Dal, the Shiv Sena, the Hindu Vishwa Parishad, the Bharatiya Janata Party and its progenitor, the Rashtriya Swayamsevak Sangh, exposing their vandalism, their penchant for violence and their pathological hatred of Muslims.

While his prose was limpid and lyrical, Dom's verse was not easy to read. His words had resonance, but one had to read every line two or three times before one could comprehend its meaning—people brought up on simple rhyming verse such as 'Twinkle, twinkle, little star' would likely find Dom's poems difficult. One could, however, detect a few themes that recurred consistently in his poems: he was obsessed with death; the hawk was the symbol of doom; his mother's insanity haunted him all his life; and he sought escape in hard liquor and making love. He summed it up in 'A Letter':

> *My father hugging me so hard it hurt,*
> *My mother mad, and time we went away.*
>
> *We travelled, and I looked for love too young.*
> *More travel, and I looked for lust instead.*
> *I was not ruled by wanting: I was young,*
> *And poems grew like maggots in my head...*

When Dom was stricken with cancer, he refused to undergo chemotherapy. It was as if he almost wallowed in the prospect of an early end, with the ghost of his insane mother hovering over him.

> *From a heavenly asylum, shrivelled Mummy,*
> *glare down like a gargoyle at your only son.*
> *...That I'm terminally ill hasn't been much help.*
> *There is no reason left for anything to exist.*
> *Goodbye now. Don't try to meddle with this.*

Dom Moraes died in his sleep on the evening of Wednesday, 2 June 2004, and was buried in the Sewri Christian Cemetery in Bombay. He was only sixty-six. He was the best Indian poet of the English language, and the greatest writer of felicitous prose.

AMIR KHUSRAU
(1253–1325)

Scholar, swordsman, poet, composer of music, inventor of the sitar and chronicler of events—all in one was Abul Hasan Amir Khusrau. He could walk the razor's edge serving both God and Mammon: he was as at home in the court of sultans as in a dervish hermitage, a flatterer of kings and the chosen disciple of a saint who avoided kings like the plague. Above all, although a first-generation Indian, he loved India and Indians more than any other country or people. Amir Khusrau is by all accounts one of the most fascinating characters of medieval Indian history. Abul Hasan's father, Saifuddin Mohammad, was a Turk of the Lachin tribe who fled from his hometown Kush in fear of the Mongols and sought asylum in Delhi, then ruled by a fellow Turk, Iltutmish. Saifuddin was a reputed swordsman. He was given employment and, in recognition of his services, granted a jagir in Patiala (Mominabad) in Uttar Pradesh. Saifuddin married the daughter of Nawab Imad-ul-Mulk, a convert from Hinduism. They had three sons, of whom the youngest, born in 1253 CE, was named Abul Hasan.

According to legend, literary greatness was predicted for Abul Hasan on the day of his birth. It is said that the father carried the child in its swaddling clothes to a soothsayer who pronounced: He will be a greater poet than Khaqani (then the greatest literary figure in Persia).

Khusrau's father moved from Mominabad to Delhi and found employment in the court of Ghiyasuddin Balban. Delhi then consisted of two cities: one at the citadel of Rai Pithora at Mehrauli and the other at Kilokheri. Khusrau was eight years old when he was brought to Delhi and taken to pay his respects to the Sufi saint Hazrat Nizamuddin. He refused to enter the khanqah and instead composed the following lines:

> Great king on whose palace walls pigeons into falcons turn
> When a seeker comes to thy door should he enter or must he return?

The saint, through his occult powers, knew what troubled young Khusrau and sent the following reply:

> If thou art a true man, enter!
> For a moment let us our secrets share
> But if thou are a fool or a knave,
> Go back, do not tarry here.

Khusrau became a disciple of Nizamuddin.

A year later Khusrau's father died. His maternal grandfather became his guardian. From his mother and her father Khusrau imbibed a love for Hindi; from his paternal relatives he picked up Turkish, Arabic and Persian.

In the earlier days, he used Sultani as his nom de plume. Later he preferred Khusrau. To this name, he added the family title Amir and came to be known as Amir Khusrau.

Khusrau did not take on an ustad. Instead he studied Persian classics. Firdausi, Khaqani and Saadi (his works had begun to circulate in India) were his masters. But more than these he learned by association with a very close friend—Amir Hasan Dehlavi, who had made a name for himself in the capital.

Khusrau spent most of his time at the saint's khanqah at Ghiyaspur on the Yamuna. Thus began his dual life. His soul was claimed by the Sufi mystics; his body by his rich patrons.

It was no easy matter to serve a saint and a sultan at the same time—particularly a saint like Nizamuddin who forbade his followers from entering government service and openly spurned the authority of the king. It was a tribute to Khusrau's genius that he remained the closest of Nizamuddin's disciples and the highest paid poet laureate of his time. Khusrau knew the art of durbardari, the art, as he said himself, 'of weaving a false story in every reign'.

Khusrau took his first job when he was twenty years old. His patron was a nephew of Balban known popularly as Malik Chajju—a brave soldier, a lover of poetry and as generous as Hatim Tai. Khusrau flattered Chajju's vanity.

> I asked the dawn: the sun thou promised where is it?
> Up came Chajju's face and the heavens were lit.

'For two years', wrote Khusrau, 'I was in that cypress garden and refreshed his [Chajju's] court with the soft breezes that blew from the lily of my tongue'. Khusrau was not a very modest man.

His downfall came over a trivial lapse of form. The emperor's second son, Bughra Khan, who was the governor of Multan, called on Chajju. He heard Khusrau recite and was so pleased that he had a platterful of silver presented to the poet. Chajju expected his protégé to refuse the gift. Khusrau accepted it—and was promptly fired.

Khusrau did no more than describe Chajju as bad ahad (breaker of promises). He went over to Bughra Khan and began to ply both his pen and his sword in the service of his new patron. For a while he lived at Samana and then accompanied Bughra on his victorious campaign to Bengal. There he composed the *Fateh Nama*—epistle of victory.

The climate of Bengal did not suit Khusrau and he obtained leave to return to Delhi. But not for very long. His next patron was the heir-apparent Prince Mohammed, governor of Multan. Multan became the centre of culture. Poets from all over the Middle East and India flocked to the prince's court. Khusrau became the royal 'pen bearer' and then the custodian of the royal Quran. His friend, Amir Hasan Dehlavi, was appointed 'custodian of the royal inkpot'. The prince sent an invitation to Sheikh Saadi along with some poems of Khusrau whom he described as Saadi-i-Hind. The sheikh praised Khusrau's work but regretted his inability to come to India.

Khusrau spent five years in Multan, 'watering the city's five rivers' as he said with characteristic immodesty with the 'seas of my delectable verses'.

In a skirmish with the Mongols, Prince Mohammed fell, his father, Emperor Balban, died of grief. Khusrau and Amir Hasan Dehlavi were taken prisoners. For the next two years Khusrau and his friend suffered the indignities of slavery in Herat and Balkh. But Khusrau continued to write. Among the compositions of the time was an elegy (marsiah) on the death of Prince Mohammed. The marsiah became the most popular song of mourning among those who had lost their kin in battle.

Khusrau escaped to return home to Mominabad. There, says he, his aged mother's breasts filled with milk at the joy of reunion with her son.

Khusrau's next patron was a chieftain of Awadh. He was as generous as Khusrau liked his patrons to be.

> I told the sea, 'You are open handed as my master.'
> The sea trembling to its very soul protested 'No! No!
> My miserable waves cast off flotsam and worthless weed.
> Your master, proud and generous, scatters rubies.'

Neither munificence nor appreciation could keep Khusrau away too long from his beloved city, Delhi, where 'handsome youths flaunted turbans tilted at roguish angles'. So two years later Khusrau was back in Delhi writing fulsome eulogies in praise of the philistine Sultan Kaikobad. He was rewarded with a khilaat and 2,000 pieces of silver. And once again Khusrau was at home at Nizamuddin's hermitage at Ghiyaspur and the 'whore-packed city', as the chronicler Barani describes Delhi.

Kaikobad debauched himself to his grave in three years. Jalaluddin Khilji ousted the Turkish oligarchy and crowned himself Sultan of Delhi. Khusrau found it convenient to forget his Turkish paternity and emphasize instead the Indian half of his blood. He wrote in praise of the new sultan. Writes Barani: 'While wine-servers brought goblets and beautiful courtesans danced, verses of Khusrau were sung.'

During his service with Jalaluddin, Khusrau had many awkward moments. Once when his first patron Malik Chajju was brought in chains to court, and again when Nizamuddin flatly refused to receive the sultan. 'My hermitage has two doors,' replied the saint. 'If the sultan enters by one, I will leave by the other.' When Jalaluddin threatened to pay a surprise visit to the khanqah at Ghiyaspur, Nizamuddin left Delhi for Pakpattan where his pir, Sheikh Farid, lived.

We do not know how Khusrau faced Malik Chajju, but when

directly confronted with a choice between the sultan and the saint, he did not hesitate to cast his lot with the latter. 'If I disobeyed the sultan I would have lost my head, but if I am false to my pir I will lose my faith,' he said.

Jalaluddin forgave Khusrau. Khusrau complimented him with even greater praise. But no sooner had the sultan's nephew Alauddin Khilji succeeded in assassinating his uncle and usurping the throne, Khusrau tuned his honeyed tongue to sing praises of the new monarch: 'Was I not the first to felicitate you on your accession? Hearken to my prophetic words! Destiny itself has made you Sultan of Delhi.'

In Alauddin's regime Khusrau's unbounded genius for eulogy blossomed to its fullness. He remained as immodest as ever, 'sprinkling the royal carpet with my charming odes'. And well-calculated: 'grass grows only with rain and poetry with the generosity of kings'. But Khusrau was getting old and finding it very tedious to waste several hours of the day hanging about the court. 'I have to string pearls and have a fresh mind to coin subtle phrases. If I have to stand before you all day and all night, how can I write poetry? Before I find a pearl worthy of your royal ear my blood must come to the boil.'

Khusrau's best work in Alauddin's regime was on the romance (ashiqa) between Prince Khizr and Deval Rani. Khusrau did not like Alauddin's favourite, Malik Kafur, who later assassinated the king. For a short while Khusrau attended the durbar of the transvestite Mubarak Khilji. By then relations between the court and Nizamuddin had come to a breaking point; Khusrau attended on both.

He discreetly absented himself in the months of turmoil when Mubarak Khilji was murdered by Khusrau Khan—who in his turn was destroyed by Ghiyasuddin Tughlaq. But as soon as the Tughlaqs had gained control of the empire, Khusrau was there to pay them homage.

Ghiyasuddin Tughlaq resented Nizamuddin. Khusrau continued to serve both. He was with the king in Bengal when Tughlaq wrote a haughty note to Nizamuddin threatening to expel him when he returned to the capital. 'Hunooz Dilli door ast. (It's a long way to Delhi),' replied the saint with prophetic foresight. And, for Ghiyasuddin, Delhi did prove to be an impossible distance. He was crushed to death under an arched gateway.

A few days later Nizamuddin was himself laid to rest. His parting words to his followers included a message for Khusrau. The poet was not to be allowed to come too close to Nizamuddin's grave lest he (Nizamuddin) be tempted to rise to embrace him.

The grief-stricken Khusrau came to Ghiyaspur and wept copious tears beside the kewra tree from where he watched his beloved saint's tomb.

> On her bed sleeps she who was once so fair
> Her face is now covered under her hair
> O, Khusrau, 'tis time thou too the homeward path did tread
> Shades of twilight over the land are spread.

A short while later (in 1325) Khusrau followed his saint into the other world. His body was buried a few metres away from the tomb of his spiritual mentor.

Khusrau loved India for its bananas, birds and betel. He also admired Indians. He enumerated ten reasons to prove the Indian's superiority over other people: Indians learn the sciences of other countries while other countries are ignorant of Indian sciences; Indians can speak foreign languages whereas foreigners never try to learn Indian languages; people come from all over the world to India to learn, but no Brahmin has to go anywhere else to educate himself; the Arab numerical system, especially the symbol zero, is of Indian origin. *Kalila wa Dimna* (Panchatantra in Arabic) was originally written in India; chess was invented in India; these three arts, the moral fable, mathematics and chess are India's contribution to universal civilization; Indian music is warm and moving and difficult to master; Indian music charms animals as well as human beings; and, finally, no other land can boast a poet like Khusrau.

However, Khusrau was not consistent in his admiration of India and Indians. He confessed that he loved India because 'the land has been saturated with the water of the sword and the vapours of infidelity have been dispersed'. Often his irritation with the people made him explode: 'Do not count Hindus among men for they venerate the cow, regard the crow superior to the parrot and read omens in the braying of an ass.'

R. K. LAXMAN
(1921–2015)

Long before I got to know him, I had sensed that Laxman had a touch of genius. I had sent a story, 'Man, How does the Government of India Run?' to the then editor of the *Illustrated Weekly of India*, C. R. Mandy. He sent the story to Laxman for a suitable illustration. Without ever having seen me or my photograph, Laxman drew a caricature of a Sikh clerk (who was the main character of my story) and it bore a startling resemblance to me.

By then he had established a reputation of being India's best cartoonist and most people took the *Times of India* because of his front page cartoons and its last page crossword puzzle. The rest of the paper was like any other national daily. However distinguished its editors, few people bothered with the contents of its edit page.

I knew Laxman was the youngest of R. K. Narayan's six brothers. His illustrations of his brother's short stories put life into the narrative and highlighted the fact that they were Tamil Brahmins settled in Mysore. We struck up a close friendship almost from the first day I took up the editorship of the *Illustrated Weekly of India*. I told him that in my opinion he was the world's greatest cartoonist. I meant it because I had lived in England, the USA and France for many years and seen the works of cartoonists there.

Laxman did not protest: he evidently agreed with my assessment of his worth. Almost every other morning he came to my room and asked me to order coffee for him. He never bothered to ask me if I was busy. Far from resenting his dropping in unannounced, I looked forward to the gossip sessions. However, while he thought nothing of wasting my time every other morning, he never allowed anyone to enter his cabin while he was at work.

Laxman was as witty a raconteur of people's foibles as he was adept in sketching them on paper. I discovered that he was a bit of a snob and did not deign to talk to the junior staff. My son, Rahul, once told me that he had run into Laxman at a cinema. When Laxman discovered that Rahul was not in the most expensive seats, he ticked him off.

He was a great socializer and could be seen at the cocktail parties of consulates, the rich and the famous. He loved driving through congested streets and gladly accepted my invitations for drinks, driving all the way from Malabar Hill where he lived, to Colaba, five miles away from my flat. Unlike his brother who was abstemious, Laxman loved his Scotch. It had to be of premium quality. However, he never returned the hospitality.

Other characteristics I noticed about him, which he shared with his brother, was an exaggerated respect for money. Laxman and I were asked by Manjushri Khaitan of the B. K. Birla family to produce commemoration volumes on Calcutta's 300th anniversary. We were given five-star accommodation. I accepted whatever Manjushri offered me for writing the text. Laxman demanded and got twice as much. His cartoons sold many more copies than my book did.

Underneath the facade of modesty, both Narayan and Laxman conceal enormous amounts of self-esteem and inflated egos. Once again, I have to concede that neither has anything to be modest about. They are at the top in their respective fields.

V. S. NAIPAUL
(b. 1932)

When I got the news of V. S. Naipaul being awarded the Nobel Prize in Literature, I was delighted and felt that I had been vindicated. I was delighted because I have known him as a friend for over thirty-five years. I have met his first wife, who was English, and get on famously with his charming, vivacious present wife, Nadira, who is Pakistani Punjabi. I met his late brother, Shiva, and saw quite a lot of his mother when she visited Delhi. Whether it was in Delhi or Bombay, throwing a party for Vidia was a must. I took him with me wherever I went. He liked being entertained and meeting new people. He never returned the hospitality. That did not matter as everyone felt privileged to have him in their house and to be able to drop his name.

I feel vindicated because every time I wrote about him, I said he deserved the Nobel Prize in Literature as he was a much better writer than many other Nobel laureates. He handled the English language with greater finesse than any contemporary writer and his range of interests was wider: humour, history, travelogues, religion, the clash of civilizations, personal profiles. Why the coveted prize eluded him for so long I could only attribute to some kind of deep-seated prejudice against writers who did not write in their mother tongue or to political considerations. Although Naipaul is a Trinidad-born Hindu, English is his mother tongue and he is essentially an objective observer of political movements, bold enough to come to his own conclusions.

When I first met Naipaul, I had only read his *A House for Mr Biswas*. I sensed then that a new star had risen in the literary firmament. That book has remained my top favourite. I can't recall exactly how we met. Perhaps he rang me up from his hotel and I invited him and his English wife over to my home. I became his escort in Delhi. He was a shy man of few words. His wife was even shyer and hardly spoke. It was evident that they were not enjoying their visit to the land of his forefathers. She was under the weather, bothered by the heat, dust and pestilence of flies. One early morning I took them to Surajkund. We stood on a ridge, looking at the rock-strewn valley ablaze with flame of the forest in flower. Vidia looked at the scene for a long time. I thought I would read a memorable description of it in his next book. Then I took him to Tughlaqabad. I had brought sandwiches and coffee. As we sat munching our sandwiches, village urchins gathered around us. They had nothing but loincloths to cover their nakedness. Their eyes and noses were running and they had flies all over their faces. In *An Area of Darkness*, Naipaul dismissed the bewitching scene of the flame of the forest trees in flower in a couple of lines but had more to say about the semi-naked urchins with flies around their eyes. It was the same with his visit to Kashmir. He visited Pamposh on a moonlit night. He had less to say about the autumn crocus (saffron) scent pervading the atmosphere and more about Kashmiri women lifting their pherans and squatting to defecate. Squalor and stench attracted his attention more than scenic beauty and fragrance.

Naipaul could be very edgy. Once when I invited him to my flat to meet a few friends over drinks, he seemed to be getting on famously with an attractive Parsi lady. But as soon as she fished out a camera from her bag and asked, 'Do you mind if I take a photograph?' Vidia snapped back sourly: 'As a matter of fact, I do mind.' The poor woman was squashed. It took some time for the others to resume conversation.

At another time the owner of a big industrial house invited me to a cocktail reception at the Taj in Bombay. I took Naipaul and my son, Rahul, who had become closer to him than I was. When we entered the ballroom on time, there were very few guests who had arrived. But seated in a row were a few attractive girls. We made a beeline for them. I introduced Vidia and my son to them. None of them spoke English, nor were they related to our hosts. It transpired that they were call girls, invited for the amusement of the guests. For Naipaul, it was an insight into the methods adopted to promote business here.

Naipaul's *Among the Believers: An Islamic Journey* caused a lot of uneasiness among Muslims. Even Salman Rushdie accused him of harbouring anti-Muslim feelings. What Naipaul wrote cannot be faulted. He observed that people who accepted Islam wrote off their pre-Islamic past. This phenomenon can be verified in Muslim countries today. In Egypt, the Pharaonic period which produced the pyramids, the Sphinx and many beautiful temples is only of historic interest, bringing in tourists and foreign exchange. It is the same in Pakistan. They have consigned their Hindu and Buddhist past to archives, museums and history books. Even the period of Sikh dominance is brushed aside as of little consequence. The destruction of the Buddhas in Bamiyan is a recent example of erasing a pre-Islamic past. This can be seen in all Muslim nations, including the most westernized ones like Turkey, Morocco and Tunisia. Naipaul did not invent this fact of history; he only exposed it.

I had the opportunity of interviewing Naipaul with Bhaichand Patel on 8 May 2000. He doesn't relish being interviewed. Patel and I were very exercised over the destruction of the Babri Masjid and heckled him for what was widely believed to be the Sangh Parivar's view of the act of vandalism. Naipaul stood his ground. He was an outside observer not concerned with the rights or wrongs of destroying a mosque. The phrase he used was explanatory: 'It was a balancing of history.' I interpreted this to imply that deep in the Hindu psyche was the resentment that Muslim invaders had destroyed hundreds of their temples. So what was so devilish about destroying a dilapidated old mosque?

Ever since Naipaul married the highly animated and attractive Nadira, he has mellowed a great deal. He is not as gruff and edgy as he was. And for good reason is writing about sex with remarkable candour and erotic artistry. His latest work, *Half a Life*, has a few memorable episodes of lusty encounters between men and women other than their spouses.

Most writers who have won the Nobel Prize tend to rest on their laurels and write little of any significance thereafter. I hope this does not happen to Sir Vidia Naipaul.

FAIZ AHMED FAIZ
(1911–1984)

Faiz Ahmed Faiz was a few years senior to me in Government College, Lahore, but I did not get to know him then as I was not admitted to the select coterie of Urdu savants at the time.

He was studying for master's degrees in English and Arabic. Though a student, he had been admitted to the charmed circle of Lahore's Aesthetics Club comprising Professor A. S. Bokhari (Patras), Imtiaz Ali Taj, Taseer and Sufi Tabassum. That was due to his reputation as an up-and-coming poet. He had been composing poetry ever since he was sixteen and at his first public appearance at a mushaira in Murray College, Sialkot, from where he had taken a bachelor's degree, he had made his mark with a couplet:

Lab bund hain saaqi, mere aankhon ko pilaa
Voh jam jo minnatkash-e-sebha mahin hota

My lips are sealed, saaqi, let these eyes of mine take a sip
Without drawing to ask for wine.

It was during 1939-1945, when he was a lieutenant colonel in the British Indian Army, that I was able to persuade him to come to my home.

He was a kindly, soft-spoken man and a heavy drinker. I have not known another man drink from sunrise to sunset without showing the slightest sign of drunkenness. After Partition, I saw a lot more of him when I visited Rawalpindi. When he happened to be in Delhi I managed to get him to spend an evening in my home. By then, I had read quite a bit of his poetry in the original and the excellent translations by Victor Kiernan.

He had been put in prison many times for his trenchant criticism of dictatorial regimes and wrote some of his most moving poetry in prison. He had ardent admirers who included his jailers and their wives. I have no doubt they took good care of him. Another enigma about him was that while he lived in princely comfort himself, most of his poetry was devoted to highlighting the abysmal poverty of the downtrodden masses exhorting them to revolt and claim their God-given right to a better life. A line of doggerel about him went somewhat like this: 'Faiz ik baraa shair hai, chaman mein reh kar maarey veeraney kee gaand.' (Faiz is a great poet, he lives in a garden and buggers the wild wastes.) As in the case of many other great poets, so too in Faiz's, it was after his verses were put to music and sung that they gained popularity. My friend, the late Kingsley Martin, editor of the *New Statesman* and *Nation*, told me that once when he was visiting Lahore, Faiz took him to the prostitutes' quarters, Heera Mandi. There the girls sang Faiz's ghazals and instead of asking for money loaded Faiz with gifts as they chucked him under his chin. The most famous lines of Faiz which appear first in all his compositions run as follows:

Raat yoon dil mein teyree khoee huee yaad aayee
Jaisey veeraaney mein chupkey say bahaar aa jaaye;
Jaisey sehraaon mein hauley sey chaley baad-e-naseem
Jaisey beemaar ko bewajeh qaraar aa jaaye

Last night your memory stole into my mind
As stealthily as spring steals into a deserted wilderness
As in desert wastes a gentle breeze begins to blow,
As in the sick beyond hope, hope begins to grow.

A few years later, when I returned from England and made my home in Lahore, we resumed our acquaintance. Following the instructions of the Communist Party of India, Faiz had joined the British Army and wore an officer's uniform. It was about this time that Alys, whose elder sister was married to Taseer, came to India to marry Harkirat Singh (later a general) to whom she had been engaged while he was a cadet at Sandhurst. By then Harkirat had been married off to a Sikh girl. Alys was heart-broken. On the rebound she married Faiz and bore him two daughters: Saleema and Muneeza.

Faiz was no lady-killer. He was of short stature with a dark brown

Writers/Artists

complexion which looked as if it had been massaged with oil. He was a man of few words, soft-spoken and impassive. It was not his conversation but his poetry that made him the centre of attraction at every party. He was remarkably free of any kind of prejudice, racial or religious. Many of his closest friends were Hindus and Sikhs. He was a humanist in the best sense of the word. There were many contradictions in his character. In his writings he championed the cause of the poor and the downtrodden; his style of living was that of an aristocrat: his daily consumption of premium brands of Scotch and imported cigarettes would have fed a worker's family for a month. However, he readily deprived himself of these luxuries to live on rations of dry bread and water given to him when he was in prison.

The partition of India left deep wounds on Faiz's mind. Although he decided to stay on in the country where he was born, he refused to accept the division between the people and remained to the end of his days Pakistani, Indian and Bangladeshi. He had as little patience with national divisions as he had for the racial or the religious. He was a Communist but more at ease among capitalists, a man who denied God and yet was most God-fearing.

No sooner was Pakistan founded than Faiz found himself deep in trouble. He had a stint as editor of the *Pakistan Times* till he, along with Sajjad Zaheer and some army officers, was arrested and charged with treason. It was during his trial in the Rawalpindi conspiracy case that the chief prosecutor Habibullah, who represented the government in court by day, would visit Faiz in prison in the evening to chant Faiz's compositions to him. Faiz received a sentence of seven years' imprisonment. While serving his sentence in Hyderabad (Sind) jail he fell seriously ill and was removed to a Karachi hospital for treatment. The lady superintendent of the hospital risked her job, her reputation and her neck to whisk Faiz away to her home for a night to feed him and minister to his needs in exchange for listening to him recite his own poetry. The years in jail brought out the best of him as a poet. Being in prison, he once said, was like falling in love again:

Bujha jo rauzan-e-zindaan to dil yeh samjha hai
Ke teyree maang sitaron say bhar gaee hogee,

Chamak uthey hain silasil, to ham nay jaanan hai
Kay a sahar teyrey rukh par bikhar gaee hogee

When the light in my prison window fades and comes the night
I think of your dark tresses and stars twinkling in the parting
When the chains that bind me sparkle in the light
I see your face lit up with the light of the morning

Faiz came to India and wherever he went he received an enthusiastic welcome. People who could not read Urdu knew his poems by heart and chanted them in chorus as he recited them at their behest. It was not the honours he received, not the Lenin Peace Prize, the Lotus Award nor the honorary doctorates heaped on him but the man he was and the sort of poetry he wrote that endeared him to millions of people of the subcontinent. He was the most lovable of men.

I have little doubt that Faiz had a premonition of his death. How else can anyone interpret the last poem that he wrote?

Ajal key haath koee aa rahaa hai parwaanah
Na jaaney aaj kee fehrist main raqam kya hai

Death has some ordinance in its hand
I know not whose names are on its list today

Faiz's village of nativity, Kala Qadir, where he intended to spend his last days has renamed itself Faiz Nagar. Faiz could not have asked for a better imam zamin for his journey into the ultimate.

FAMILY AND FRIENDS

DAADIMAA

(1875–1939)

My grandmother, like everybody's grandmother, was an old woman. She had been old and wrinkled for the twenty years that I had known her. People said that she had once been young and pretty and had even had a husband, but that was hard to believe. My grandfather's portrait hung above the mantelpiece in the drawing room. He wore a big turban and loose-fitting clothes. His long white beard covered the best part of his chest and he looked at least a hundred years old. He did not look the sort of person who would have a wife or children. He looked as if he could only have lots and lots of grandchildren. As for my grandmother being young and pretty, the thought was almost revolting. She often told us of the games she used to play as a child. That seemed quite absurd and undignified on her part and we treated it like the tales of the prophets she used to tell us.

She had always been short and fat and slightly bent. Her face was a criss-cross of wrinkles running from everywhere to everywhere. No, we were certain she had always been as we had known her. Old, so terribly old that she could not have grown older, and had stayed at the same age for twenty years.

She could never have been pretty; but she was always beautiful. She hobbled about the house in spotless white with one hand resting on her waist to balance her stoop and the other telling the beads of her rosary. Her silver locks were scattered untidily over her pale, puckered face, and her lips constantly moved in inaudible prayer. Yes, she was beautiful. She was like the winter landscape in the mountains, an expanse of pure white serenity breathing peace and contentment.

My grandmother and I were good friends. My parents left me with her when they went to live in the city and we were constantly together. She used to wake me up in the morning and get me ready for school. She said her morning prayer in a monotonous sing-song while she bathed and dressed me in the hope that I would listen and get to know it by heart. I listened because I loved her voice but never bothered to learn it. Then she would fetch my wooden slate which she had already washed and plastered with yellow chalk, a tiny earthen ink pot and a reed pen, tie them all in a bundle and hand it to me. After a breakfast of a thick, stale chapatti with a little butter and sugar spread on it, we went to school. She carried several stale chapattis with her for the village dogs.

My grandmother always went to school with me because the school was attached to the temple. The priest taught us the alphabet and the morning prayer. While the children sat in rows on either side of the veranda singing the alphabet or the prayer in a chorus, my grandmother sat inside reading the scriptures. When we had both finished, we would walk back together. This time the village dogs would meet us at the temple door. They followed us to our home growling and fighting each other for the chapattis we threw to them.

When my parents were comfortably settled in the city, they sent for us. That was a turning point in our friendship. Although we shared the same room, my grandmother no longer came to school with me. I used to go to an English school in a motorbus. There were no dogs in the streets and she took to feeding sparrows in the courtyard of our city house. As the years rolled by, we saw less of each other. For some time she continued to wake me up and get me ready for school. When I came back, she would ask me what the teacher had taught me. I would tell her English words and little things of Western science and learning, the law of gravity, Archimedes' principle, the world being round, etc. This made her unhappy. She could not help me with my lessons. She did not believe in the things they taught at the English school and was distressed that there was no teaching about God and the scriptures. One day I announced that we were being given music lessons. She was very disturbed. To her, music had lewd associations. It was the monopoly of harlots and beggars and not meant for gentle folk. She rarely talked to me after that.

When I went up to university, I was given a room of my own. The common link of friendship was snapped. My grandmother accepted her seclusion with resignation. She rarely left her spinning wheel to talk to anyone. From sunrise to sunset she sat by her wheel spinning and reciting prayers. Only in the afternoon she relaxed for a while to feed the sparrows. While she sat in the veranda breaking the bread into little bits, hundreds of little birds collected around her creating a veritable bedlam of chirruping. Some came and perched on her legs, others on her shoulders. Some even sat on her head. She smiled but never shooed them away. It used to be the happiest half-hour of the day for her.

When I decided to go abroad for further studies, I was sure my grandmother would be upset. I would be away for five years, and at her age, one could never tell. But my grandmother could. She was not even sentimental. She came to see me off at the railway station but did not talk or show any emotion. Her lips moved in prayer, her mind was lost in prayer. Her fingers were busy telling the beads of her rosary. Silently she kissed my forehead, and when I left I cherished the moist imprint as perhaps the last sign of physical contact between us. But that was not so. After five years I came back home and was met by her at the station. She did not look a day older. She still had no time for words, and while she clasped me in her arms I could hear her reciting her prayers. Even on the first day of my arrival, her happiest moments were with her sparrows whom she fed for longer and with frivolous rebukes.

In the evening a change came over her. She did not pray. She collected the women of the neighbourhood, got an old drum and started to sing. For several hours she thumped the sagging skins of the dilapidated drum and sang of the homecoming of warriors. We had to persuade her to stop, to avoid overstraining. That was the first time since I had known her that she did not pray.

The next morning she was taken ill. It was a mild fever and the doctor told us that it would go. But my grandmother thought differently. She told us that her end was near. She said that since only a few hours before the close of the last chapter of her life she had omitted to pray, she was not going to waste any more time talking to us.

We protested. But she ignored our protests. She lay peacefully in bed, praying and telling her beads. Even before we could suspect, her lips stopped moving and the rosary fell from her lifeless fingers. A peaceful pallor spread on her face and we knew that she was dead.

It was the summer of 1939.

We lifted her off the bed and, as is customary, laid her on the ground and covered her with a red shroud. After a few hours of mourning we left her alone to make arrangements for her funeral.

In the evening we went to her room with a crude stretcher to take her to be cremated. The sun was setting and had lit her room and veranda with a blaze of golden light. We stopped halfway in the courtyard. All over the veranda and in her room right up to where she lay, dead and stiff, wrapped in the red shroud, thousands of sparrows sat scattered on the floor. There was no chirping. We felt sorry for the birds and my mother fetched some bread for them. She broke it into little crumbs, the way my grandmother used to, and threw it to them. The sparrows took no notice of the bread. When we carried my grandmother's corpse off, they flew away quietly. Next morning the sweeper swept the breadcrumbs into the dustbin.

SOBHA SINGH
(1890–1978)

I was in Bombay when my father died in Delhi. My relations with my parents were like those that exist in traditional Indian families. Rigid rules of courtesy were observed, but no confidences were exchanged. He did not have any favourite among his four sons. Perhaps I came closest to being one, but I had disappointed him by not being the conventional success he had hoped for. Like most fathers, he had a soft spot for his only daughter whom he plied with gifts and to whom he left an unencumbered estate bigger than the portions he gave his sons. My mother distinctly favoured her youngest son, Daljit. A bitter quarrel had arisen between my eldest and youngest brother. My mother had never liked my eldest brother's wife and blatantly sided with Daljit. I knew nothing about my brothers' falling out over the division of property and dragging each other to court till my father wrote to me and asked me to come over. I was mortified to learn about the trivial issues they were wrangling over. My uncle, Ujjal Singh, had tried to arbitrate between the two and failed. I took over the unpleasant job. While Daljit appeared more amenable to reason on the surface, he broke his solemn promise given in writing to me by taking over a joint society when his eldest brother was away. I confronted him in front of my parents and angrily rebuked him of being a dagabaaz (betrayer). He broke down. He swore by his mother—he was always swearing by her—that he would not do it again. I tore up the proceedings of the meeting in which he had assumed control of the enterprise and succeeded in making a mutually acceptable partition between them.

Relations between my parents underwent a sea change over the years. For years my father had laid down the law with a heavy hand. As he began to get older and hard of hearing, his dependence on his wife increased. She began to tick him off for making people repeat whatever they had said—hain? kee kyaah?—and being clumsy. He dropped food on his tie and coat while eating. He no longer lost his temper but submitted meekly to being put in his place. Whenever I visited him, he asked me to read the papers to him and solicited my opinion on important events. He was never one for exercise: walking up and down his lawn was all he did to keep himself fit. He also observed no dietary rules. He had a large breakfast of cornflakes, eggs, sausages, toast and honey, and tea. He had a couple of gins before lunch; for afternoon tea he took slices of cake, biscuits or Indian sweets. He took two to three Scotches before dinner and often brandy afterwards.

Dinner consisted of at least four or five courses: soup, fish, meat, vegetable and pudding. When travelling, he ate whatever was available on railway platforms. On his way to Mashobra by car he sampled the pickles at a dhaba four miles up the road from Kalka and ate pedas at Jablee. He never put on weight and remained slim to the last. He was a great one for taking pills—to whip up appetite, to digest what he had eaten. He had several operations—for kidney stones, cataract, piles and hernia. One thing he never missed was his sleep. No sooner did he put his head on the pillow than he was lost to the world. More than anything else, it was sound sleep that sustained him for ninety years.

It was sad to see him age and become frail. I made it a point to come to Delhi every fortnight and spend an hour with him in the mornings and either have my evening Scotch with him or get him over to dine with us. The last time I saw him alive, he looked frailer than ever, and was evidently aware that he did not have many days left. When I was taking my leave he asked me when I planned to come to Delhi next. I told him I would be back in a fortnight. 'Fortnight?' he asked. And said no more.

A week later my wife rang me to say he was not well and she was going over to see him. An hour later she rang again to say he was much better and she had had a drink with him. My mother and sister were with him. A few minutes later, she rang a third time to tell me he was dead. This was at 8.30 p.m. on 18 April 1978.

I was numb. For a long time I sat still not knowing what to do. Then I rang up the Zakarias and asked Fatma if she could tell Rahul and put us on the early morning flight to Delhi. She never failed me in a crisis. A few minutes later the Zakarias came over to see me. After half an hour I asked them to leave me so that I could get some sleep.

I got no sleep that night. I kept going over events in my father's life. A self-made man, a generous father whom I had barely known as a person with human failings. I knew full well that if it had not been for his constant support, I would never have been able to write a single book.

Having once been the biggest builder of New Delhi, his death made the front pages of all the daily papers. There was a large turnout at his cremation and an even larger one filling the entire lawn of Sujan Singh Park at his last obsequial ceremony. I was asked by my brothers to make the final oration. Fortunately I was able to say my piece without breaking down.

Nishaan-e-mard-e-momin ba too goyam?
Choon marg aayad, tabassum bar lab-e-ost

You ask me about the signs of a man of faith?
When death comes to him, he has a smile on his lips.

(Allama Iqbal)

My father did better than face death with a smile; he had a glass of Scotch in his hand a few minutes before he laid himself on his deathbed.

VEERAN BAI
(c.1899-1985)

Of my parents, I felt more relaxed with my mother than with my father. None of her children were as scared of her as we were of our father. When we were small, she often threatened to slap us, but it never went beyond raising her hand and threatening 'maaraan chaat?' Nothing followed. She was frail, short, with little confidence in herself. Whatever little she may have had as a girl was squashed by her overbearing husband who would not trust her to run her home. He even prepared menus for his dinner parties—they hardly ever varied from tomato soup, fish, chicken, pilaf, followed by pudding—and he kept all the accounts except the dhobi's. There were other reasons for her willing subservience to her husband—her father and two brothers were in our employment; of her three sisters' husbands, two depended on my father's patronage. She had never been to school and only learned Gurmukhi to be able to write letters and read the headlines of Punjabi newspapers. She didn't waste time on books and preferred to gossip with her sisters and maidservant, Bhajno, who was an inveterate carrier of tales against her sons' wives. However, when I was abroad I got more news from the few lines she wrote to me in Gurmukhi than the two pages of typescript my father dictated to his secretary. He wrote about the government, political wrangling and the budget; she wrote about births, liaisons, marriages and deaths. She often grumbled that she could not read or write English. Despite the instructors my father employed to teach her the language, she stubbornly refused to go beyond 'yes, no, good morning, good night, goodbye and thank you'.

When the Punjabi translation of my novel *Train to Pakistan* was published, I gave her the first copy. I did not expect her to read it. When I went to see her next morning, my father told me that she had been reading the novel late into the night and was down with a severe headache. I went to her bedroom. She was lying covered from head to foot in her shawl. I shook her by the shoulder and asked how she was feeling. She peeped out of the shawl with one eye and made a one-word comment: 'Beysharam!' (shameless creature).

My mother was something of a hypochondriac. The only thing she really suffered from were migraine headaches. The attacks could be so severe that she had to stay in bed for two days and only felt better after she had thrown up a few times. But whenever she caught a cold she was sure it was her last moment. Whenever she felt a pain in any part of her body she was sure it was cancer. She had heard that cancer was incurable. Therefore what she had could be nothing except cancer. When my father died in his ninetieth year, she was in her eighties and in good health. Instead of being shattered by his going, as everyone expected, she came into her own as a very domineering materfamilias. Nobody dared to address her except as Lady Sobha Singh. Like Queen Victoria, she held court every day. At eleven she presided over the mid-morning coffee session; in the evening, over drinks and dinner. I persuaded her to have a little alcohol in the evenings. At first she consumed it surreptitiously. When bearers came round with tray loads of soft drinks for the ladies at parties she would tell them that her son was bringing her orange juice. I initially spiked her glass with a little gin, and then I introduced her to Scotch. Again she made a mild protest. 'What will people say! An old, illiterate woman from a village drinking whisky?' She began to like her sundowner and became discerning enough to tell good Scotch from bad desi.

In her ninetieth year she began to sense that she did not have very much longer to live. She never said anything about it but started giving things away. My father's sweaters, his ebony walking stick with a silver knob, and his gold watch came to me; jewellery and a gold watch went to my sister; jewellery, watches, gold pens, gold buttons, and sovereigns were distributed among sons, daughters-in-law and their progeny. There was seldom a morning when I went to see her when she did not give me a shirt, a pair of socks or shoes that my father had worn. We knew that she meant to give these things away with her own hands.

Without there being anything specifically wrong with her, she began to wither away. Dr I. P. S. Kalra, who was married to my cousin, also a doctor, came to see her twice a day to take her blood pressure and temperature. She began to spend a longer time in bed. My sister slept in her bedroom to help her go to the bathroom. Then a night maid was hired to clean, sponge and help change her clothes. Her appearances at coffee sessions became rarer and rarer. But even when half conscious, she would send for her servant, Haria, and mumble 'Coffee'. He would assure her that visitors were being served coffee. Many times my telephone rang to tell me that she was sinking. We would hurry over. Dr Kalra would be there giving her a shot of something or the other. She then rallied round and we returned to our homes. One evening, when all her children, grandchildren and a number of great-grandchildren were there, she went into a coma from which she never recovered.

We spent many hours of many days sitting by her supine body, assured by the rise and fall of her sheet that she was still alive. More than once we asked Dr Kalra not to persist in injecting her with life-saving drugs and let her go in peace. He refused to listen to us and said that he was determined to keep her alive for as long as he could. Back in my flat, I dreaded the ringing telephone. The final call came on the afternoon of 9 March 1985. It was my sister's anguished voice crying, 'She's gone.'

By the time we got to her she looked peacefully asleep. Beside her pillow, incense spiralled upwards to the ceiling. My elder brother sat by her bedside reading out from a small prayer book. Others embraced each other in tears and sat in chairs in the garden, only to break down again and again as people came to condole them. As in earlier happenings in the family, it was my younger brother, Brigadier Gurbux Singh, who took control of the situation. He made me draft the obituary notice, corrected it and sent it off to all the Delhi papers. He fixed the time of her cremation and the day the Akhand Path would commence and terminate with bhog and kirtan. He ordered us to return to our homes for the night. He, his wife and my sister would stay with the body. My elder brother sat by her making the japs over and over again throughout the night, as he had done years earlier by our father's body.

The next morning we took our mother's body to the same electric crematorium where we had earlier taken our father and uncle. My brother, Gurbux, took her ashes to Hardwar as he had our father's ashes and those of my grandmother, to be immersed in the Ganga. Thus ended the days of Veeran Bai, Lady Sobha Singh, my mother.

RAJNI PATEL
(1915–1982)

Why do people take the life out of a full-blooded person when paying him tributes on his demise? Rajni Patel was larger than life itself, packed with ingredients both good and bad, which made him the kind of human dynamo he was. But all our wretched politicians and journalists could say about him were cliché-ridden eulogies they spout about every celebrity when he departs: great son of India, freedom fighter, great jurist etc., etc. More than liver cancer or cardiac arrest, it was these banal homilies that killed Rajni after his death.

Rajni had many lovable qualities: the gift of friendship, standing by his friends even when he knew they were in the wrong; princely generosity; love of liquor and beautiful women. He also had many shortcomings: lack of political and financial scruples; preaching what he did not practise; and calculated name-dropping. In the half century that I knew him, I saw both sides of the Rajni coin. But so strong was his affection for his friends that none of us had the courage to disown him; the best any of us could do was to slowly extricate oneself from his circle.

I first met Rajni when he was at Cambridge University. He was an ardent communist; I was not. Our dialogues always ended up in a brawl. Once he, Krishna Menon and I had to travel together to Paris. Both ignored my presence throughout the six-hour journey. When I went to live in Bombay, Rajni had ceased being a member of the Communist Party and had joined the Indira Gandhi Congress. 'We are now members of the same church,' he said to me. Thereafter we exchanged hospitality on a weekly basis.

At the time Rajni had broken with his second wife Susheila—a woman of extraordinary beauty—Nordic complexion, Hellenic features and grey-green eyes that most Chitpavan Brahmins have. Their three sons lived with the mother. Rajni had taken up with a Gujarati divorcee, Bakul Bhatt, who was almost twenty years younger than him. Susheila did not forgive him for ditching her and embarrassed him at many public meetings.

Rajni and Bakul were obviously very much in love with each other but it was at a drinking orgy many years later, with Rajni very high in his cups, that at a midnight ceremony the two were pronounced man and wife.

Rajni's rise to eminence was as spectacular as it was sinister. He had no political base whatsoever: to describe him as a labour leader is absolute hogwash; he could not have won a district board by election. It was during his tenure as president that the Bombay Pradesh Congress Committee became a kind of board of directors of an affluent company. He was the pioneer in the cult of businessmen-politicians. Rajni's methods of extracting money from the wealthy made his predecessor money-collectors S. K. Patil and Atulya Ghosh appear like novices. I recall one evening when he had invited a bevy of millionaires to raise money to help the drought-stricken in Maharashtra. With Royal Salute Scotch (₹1,500 per bottle) and French champagne, we discussed hunger and famine. As usual at every one of Rajni's parties, the discussion was interrupted many times by Bakul announcing that Rajni was wanted on the phone by the Prime Minister or some member of her Cabinet. Those who were there for the first time were very impressed.

However, there is no denying the fact that every person who was anybody sought Rajni's patronage. I cannot count the number of chief ministers, governors, millionaires, generals, admirals and politicians that I met in his apartment.

The two sides of Rajni's character were sharply etched—when one of his sons was seriously injured in a car accident, and was for many weeks in the intensive care ward of Jaslok Hospital, Rajni had a suite of rooms on the ground floor reserved to receive his shoals of visitors. They were served tea, coffee, Scotch and eats. An intercom kept them informed of the boy's condition. On my last visit to the hospital I was allowed to see the lad. On my way out, an elderly grey-haired but very handsome lady who was sitting on a stool rose and accosted me: 'Please tell me how the boy is doing,' she said. I told her, adding that she could go in and see for herself. 'I am not allowed to go in,' she replied, without any emotion. This was Susheila Patel, the boy's mother.

DHARMA KUMAR
(1928–2001)

She died early morning on Friday, 19 October 2001. She was in the intensive care unit of Apollo Hospital for over a month; so her end did not come as a surprise. What sustained a little hope in my mind was that women like Dharma did not die; they faded out of memory like a lost dream. She was seventy-three. I would add the word 'only' to the sentence because she seemed agelessly youthful. She was more animated than any woman I have ever met. I write about her because all of us have someone or the other in our lives who means more to us than we care to admit till after they are gone.

It must be over fifty years ago that I first met her and her husband, Lovraj Kumar, at a large luncheon party in a garden. He was an executive in Burma Shell; she was working on her doctoral thesis for Cambridge University. She was the centre of attraction, sparkling with wit and humour. She was an excellent mimic and delightfully malicious. She had everyone in splits of happy laughter. I was completely bowled over. For the next few days I spoke about her to everyone I knew and tried to get as much information about her and her husband as I could.

Lovraj Kumar was from Uttar Pradesh, the only child of well-known and rich parents. He was also a very bright student. He won a Rhodes scholarship to Oxford. Dharma was a Tamil Brahmin and the only child of a well-known scientist, Dr Venkatraman, who was the head of the National Chemical Laboratory in Pune. They met in England and got married. Lovraj answered all that Dharma wanted of a man. She had an exaggerated respect for academics; almost all her cousins had gained firsts in Oxford or Cambridge; Lovraj had bettered them. She did not much care for wealth. She married him because he was brighter than any of her many suitors. She, however, did not like Lovraj joining Burma Shell, becoming a boxwallah and taking orders from white sahibs. Lovraj was a soft-spoken and self-effacing man. Dharma was outgoing, garrulous and revelled in admiration.

She was not the kind of woman I usually fell for. Her features were passable; she used no make-up or perfume. It was her animation which I found irresistible. Her eyes sparkled, her toes twitched, her hands were restless. I did not have the curriculum vitae to gain entrance to Dharma's charmed circle of friends. I had a very poor academic record, had done lowly jobs and the few books I had written were not highly rated in academic circles. Come to think of it, the only reason she responded to my overtures was that she was overwhelmed by my adoration. It was an entirely one-sided affair. I dedicated my second novel, *I Shall Not Hear The Nightingale*, to her. I don't think she bothered to read it—or for that matter anything else I wrote. She treated me as a very light-weight character which I no doubt was.

We began to invite the Kumars to our small parties. Dharma was always the centre of attraction; her quiet, gentle, self-effacing husband became the greater favourite with my wife and daughter. For the next few winters the Kumars and their daughter, Radha, became members of our small group which used to set out every Sunday morning before dawn and drive twenty or thirty miles out of Delhi to explore the countryside. This group usually consisted of Evan Charlton (editor of *The Statesman*), his wife, Joy, and their daughter, Victoria; Henry Croom-Johnson (head of the British Council), and his wife, Jane; and Prem Kirpal. The most important member of the group was our German Shepherd, Simba, who was always in a high state of excitement to get out in the open country and chase rabbits, peacocks, or herds of cows. We would have our coffee and sandwiches before we set out through rough country and agricultural fields ending on the banks of the Yamuna. After two to three hours of marathon walking, we returned to our base to drink chilled beer. These winter Sunday morning walks were most exhilarating. I made it a point to be with Dharma. She was obsessed with economics; I discovered that the people she admired most were economists. I knew nothing about one or the other.

Dharma's favourite put-downs were about a cousin, Raghavan Aiyar. Like others of the family, he was a topper: first in MA philosophy from Madras; first class first in Cambridge and elected President of the Cambridge Union. While at university, he acquired a group of admirers who assembled in his room periodically to hear him speak.

He told them that the source of all human frailties was the ego. Unless one conquered one's ego, there could be no peace of mind. One day a lady admirer asked, 'I agree with all you say about the ego, but how does one conquer the ego?'

'Good question!' replied Raghavan Aiyar. 'You will appreciate it poses a bigger problem for me than it does for you. For myself I have evolved a formula for self-extinction. Every day I sit in padmasana (lotus pose), shut my eyes and repeat: 'I am not the Raghavan Aiyar who got a first class from Madras University; I am not the Raghavan Aiyar who got a first class first from Cambridge University; I am not the Raghavan Aiyar who is the most brilliant philosopher of the East; I am merely a vehicle of the mahatma, a spark of the Divine.'

According to Dharma, when Raghavan Aiyar stood for presidentship of the union, he did not bother to canvass for himself but left it to his admirers. After the counting of votes, his fans rushed to his room to break the good news. They found him seated in padmasana on his carpet with his eyes shut: 'You've won! You've won!' they shouted triumphantly. Raghavan Aiyar raised one hand with his finger pointing to the roof and exclaimed: 'Victory is Thine, O Lord!'

Dharma got her doctorate in Economics. She became a professor at the Delhi School of Economics and wrote a couple of books which were very well received by economists. Her husband left Burma Shell to become Secretary in the Petroleum Ministry of the central government. She was happy that she was no longer the wife of a boxwallah. But even as the wife of a much-respected bureaucrat, she refused to entertain ministers or befriend their wives. When compelled to meet them, because of her husband's status, she would go out of her way to belittle them.

Undeterred by her indifference, I continued to long for her company. The break came unexpectedly. We were dining with Lovraj and Dharma. Dharma had got some kind of lecturing assignment abroad. She had special venom against fake academics who managed to get invitations from foreign universities and had nothing to show for them. She casually told me of the invitation. Very light-heartedly I asked, 'Dharma, how did you wangle it?' She went pale with anger and burst out: 'I don't like that kind of insinuation. I am not a wangler.' The outburst of anger took everyone unawares. An uneasy silence descended on the table. The party was ruined.

The one thing I cannot forgive or forget is people losing their temper with me. I swore to have nothing more to do with Dharma. I did not ring her up as I used to. I think she sensed that I had been upset by her outburst of temper. But she was too proud to say sorry. She did her best to make amends but something within me had snapped which I could not join together.

After some months, our families began to see each other again. But I was never relaxed in her company. I felt more at ease with Lovraj and their daughter, Radha, than I did with Dharma.

When her husband died suddenly, I went to the crematorium, expecting to meet Dharma and wipe out the uneasiness that had come between us. She was not there. As I embraced Radha, I broke down in tears. It was Radha who consoled me.

None of us who cherished Dharma realized that her fits of temper may have been due to things going wrong inside her. She developed a brain tumour and had to be flown to London for surgery. It did not help. Another tumour developed. Then another. In her final years, the only one left to look after her was her ninety-four-year-old mother-in-law. She told everyone, 'Dharma is not my bahu (daughter-in-law) but my beti (daughter).'

She was with her to the last. It is hard for me to accept the fact that Dharma was mortal. I will not see Dharma any more. She may not have cared for me but I will cherish her memory for the years left to me.

AVEEK SARKAR
(b. 1945)

My association with *The Telegraph* is as old as *The Telegraph* itself. I started writing for it the day it was born and continue to do so till this day. It began with the 'Malice' column that I wrote for the *Hindustan Times*. The proprietor of that paper, K. K. Birla, was generous enough to allow me to offer the column to *The Telegraph*. Later, when the *Hindustan Times* started publishing in Calcutta, he quite rightly withdrew his permission. That did not break my association with the paper as it took over my other column, 'This Above All'. So I remain a part of *The Telegraph* parivar. As a matter of fact, my relationship with the Sarkar family goes back more than forty years to when I was the editor of the *Illustrated Weekly of India* in Bombay. M. J. Akbar was among the earliest trainees on my staff. So was Mallika, who later married Akbar. I was nominated godfather for their firstborn.

Aveek Sarkar who was the editor-in-chief of the Anandabazar group, used to drop in to see me whenever he was in Bombay. When I was fired from the editorship of the *Illustrated Weekly*, he and Akbar offered me the editorship of the fortnightly, *New Delhi*. I was given a swanky office in the Press Trust of India building on Parliament Street, a staff of my own choosing and a brand new car. I was on cloud nine.

The euphoria did not last very long. There were strikes in the *Anandabazar Patrika*'s press and the printing schedule went haywire. *New Delhi* often became a monthly. I threw in the towel. The Sarkars understood and folded up the journal. Our friendship remained unimpaired. On the contrary, Arup Sarkar loaded me with expensive gifts: a massive terracotta Ganpati and a large lithograph of Lord Harding receiving captured Sikh artillery in Calcutta following their victory in the first Anglo-Sikh War of 1845. It's a rare piece. The Anandabazar family, of which *The Telegraph* is a member, has done more for art and literature than any other publishing house. Many Bengali writers including Sunil Gangopadhyay and the Bangladeshi

Taslima Nasreen have been published and honoured by it. Rakhi Sarkar, Aveek's wife, has personally taken the works of artists from Calcutta to other Indian cities. I don't know of a government academy of arts and literature that has done so much.

Arup's gifts were followed by an invitation to my wife and me to attend the twenty-fifth wedding anniversary of Aveek and Rakhi at the Grand Hotel. The programme was kept as a surprise for the couple till they arrived at the banquet hall. It was a memorable feast. They also made me an adviser of Penguin/Viking (India) in which they acquired substantial shares. My home is flooded with books, thanks to the Sarkars.

The Telegraph, ever since its inception, arrives in Delhi in the evening. When it was first published and was delivered to me after sunset, I used to merely glance at it as in the morning I had to plough through half a dozen papers. But very soon I realized, despite my cursory glance at *The Telegraph*, that it was a more professional product than any of the Delhi morning dailies. It was professional in production, in printing, in layout and in its selection and placement of news. I began to read it more carefully and began enjoying it. Now it has become my staple evening read. I look forward to it with my sundowner. There are certain features of *The Telegraph* that I would like to pick out for special mention. One is that the paper does not believe in gimmicks. There are no special columns devoted to religion and spirituality; I find such columns immensely irritating. It also doesn't reproduce risqué jokes from *Playboy* or the Internet.

In a newspaper such jokes are in bad taste. It is only from *The Telegraph* that I get detailed news of eastern India and the Northeast. No other newspaper provides me with this.

The Telegraph, since its inception, has had a nose for controversy. I appreciate this even though I was once a victim of it. When I made some critical comments about Gurudev Tagore, *The Telegraph* was the only paper to splash it on the front page. As a result of this I became the subject of a censure motion in the West Bengal legislative assembly and in the Rajya Sabha. I am absolutely addicted to *The Telegraph* crossword. I find it to be about the best in the country. Neither too difficult like the one in *The Statesman* nor too silly like the ones in other papers. *The Telegraph* crossword is the perfect companion to my evening Scotch whisky.

In my long life of ninety-three years, I have worked in many government departments and edited several journals, official and privately owned. I can say without hesitation that I have never served in another business house where I received as much respect, affection and high wages as I have from the Anandabazar group, now officially named ABP Private Ltd.

Aveek has a few eccentricities that I find charming. He used to like to smoke Cuban cigars. He lit one after every meal. 'How many do you have every day?' I once asked him. A little hesitantly he replied, 'Only four.' I worked out the cost of Romeo y Julieta: ₹150 each. 'So you blow up ₹600 everyday in smoke!' He smiled sheepishly.

He still likes to entertain friends in restaurants, never at his home. Like a pukka Brit his home is his castle, impregnable. I breached its bulwark by provoking him. 'You Bengalis don't have a cuisine. Besides maachher jhol, rasgollas and mishti, you have nothing to offer. In Calcutta you can find gourmet French, Italian, Chinese, Mughlai and Marwari restaurants. Not one where you can have Bengali food.' At the time there were no Bengali restaurants in the metropolis or anywhere else in India. He gave me a very tame answer: 'We Bengalis are not restaurant-goers. We prefer to eat at home. And eat very well.'

'I have never been invited to a Bengali home,' I replied. 'In Bangladesh yes—and enjoyed the best hilsa I've ever tasted. Never in Calcutta.' That got one an invitation to the Sarkars' citadel. Rakhi went out of her way to prove there was more to Bengali cuisine than I thought.

Another of Aveek's eccentricities is to number everyone in order of merit. If I mention the name of a singer, dancer or artist, he will place them in the order of merit. 'So and so is number one, so and so number two, so and so number three.' There is no point contradicting him because he exudes so much self-confidence.

And lastly, his habit of never answering letters. David Davidar, then the head of Penguin Books India, who had to write to him officially, once said to me in a tone of exasperation, 'He has a shredder installed in his office. It can separate envelopes that contain cheques from those that do not. The chequeless envelopes and their contents go straight into the shredder without Aveek having to open them.'

PRABHA DUTT
(1944–1984)

It would have been more appropriate if Prabha had written this piece on me rather than I on her. Her pen was still rapier sharp; mine is somewhat blunted with age. She would have used royal-blue ink to write my obituary; I can only use my colourless tears to write hers. For Prabha it was not yet time for the noonday prayer; for me bells peal for evensong. None of these considerations counted with the Divine Reaper: early one morning when He set out to gather blossoms from the media's flower-bed of lilies, he plucked one still in the prime of her youth and the fairest of them all.

I knew very little of Prabha Dutt before I became her boss. She was the bossy type and instinctively resented anyone lording over her. When she first came to see me in my office she made it quite clear that she wasn't the kind of person who took orders from anyone; she knew her job better than I did and if I minded my business she would mind hers. She regarded me with her large grey eyes as an insect-collector would examine the latest beetle in his collection and put me several questions framed to find out what kind of editor I would make. I was somewhat overawed by her presence and the viva-voce test she put me through. It took me several months to break through her impersonal, no-nonsense attitude towards me and persuade her to accept the hand of friendship I extended to her.

The breakthrough was dramatic. Prabha was as much married to the *Hindustan Times* as she was to her husband and as involved with the paper as she was with her two daughters. And extremely touchy about both. It was after one of her many outbursts against a colleague who got away with very little work that she dissolved in tears of rage. I was able to take the liberty of putting a paternal arm round her shoulders. She shrugged it off but thereafter did me the honour of treating me as her father-in-office to whom she could turn in moments of crisis.

In Prabha's scheme of values, work took precedence over everything else. This gave her enormous courage to speak her mind without bothering who she was speaking to and writing without concern of consequences that might follow. In my presence she told K. K. Birla to his face what was wrong with the *Hindustan Times*. She bust financial and social rackets (she had a ladylike disdain for sex scandals) and was often threatened with violence.

The one and only time she quarrelled with me was when I tried to withhold her story on S. L. Khurana who had been an executive president of the *Hindustan Times* and was then Lieutenant Governor of Delhi. I have little doubt that if she had found out something about my evading taxes, smuggling contraband or involvement in some shady deal, despite her affection for me, she would not have spared me.

Prabha was a very conservative, strait-laced person, passionately devoted to her family, friends, servants and their families. She not only spent every moment she could spare from work teaching her own and her servants' children, but eagerly took on the problems of her friends on her own shoulders. She was as fierce in her loyalties towards people she befriended as she could be aggressively unfriendly and outspokenly offensive to their detractors. These characteristics gave her the image of one who was hard as nails and quick of temper. Those who knew her better realized how soft she really was: every outburst of temper was followed by a cascade of tears. She was like the cactus, prickly on the outside, sugar-sweet within.

Had Prabha a premonition that she had a short time to go? I am not sure. She certainly crammed in as much activity for her two daughters as any mother would who felt she may soon be parted from them. On the other hand a day before her haemorrhage she went to see a relative in hospital and told him very cheerfully how lucky he was to be lying comfortably in bed without having to bother about going to office. Little did she then know that within a few hours she would be in the same hospital fighting a losing battle for her own life. Her closest friend, Usha Rai, told me that the evening before she died, as Usha was rubbing her hands, Prabha asked her in a feeble voice: 'Are you reading the lines on my palm? Tell me, will I leave this hospital alive?'

In all my years in journalism I have yet to meet as gutsy a girl, with integrity that brooked no compromise, daring that verged on foolhardiness, total dedication to her work with contempt for the kaamchor (shirker) than Prabha Dutt. The most fitting tribute I can pay her is by placing a wreath stolen from Shakespeare:

> Now boast thee death, in thy possession lies
> A lass unparalleled!

P. C. LAL
(1916–1982)

There is a Hindustani saying that men of destiny have signs of greatness even in their infancy. No one who knew Pratap Lal in school and college spotted any such telltale signs indicating the heights to which he would rise. We became friends at Modern School when we were only five years old. Ten years later, we exchanged turbans to become dharambhais—brothers in faith. There was nothing dharmic about my intentions; though only fifteen, I was besotted with Pratap's sister, Roma, who was two years older than me. She was the heart-throb of my generation.

The Lals were a mixed Punjabi-Bengali family. Pratap's father Rai Bahadur Basant Lal, assistant commissioner of income tax, was a Punjabi, his mother was a Bengali Sarkar who spoke Punjabi fluently. In their home they spoke four languages with equal fluency: English, Hindustani, Bengali and Punjabi. They were Brahmos, more liberal in their views than most Indian families of Delhi.

The outbreak of war in 1939 rescued Pratap Lal from what might well have been an undistinguished career at the Bar. He promptly threw away his law books and joined the air force. Being familiar with the workings of aircraft he had no problem rising rapidly up the ranks. And displayed yet another unknown characteristic: bravery.

He flew dive bombers supporting General W. J. Slim's drive against the Japanese in Burma. He was awarded the Distinguished Flying Cross. When Independence came he held the rank of squadron leader. He was chosen for an advanced course in Andover and was the first pilot of the Indian Air Force to fly faster than the speed of sound.

In 1966 he was made managing director of the Hindustan Aeronautics Limited factory at Bangalore.

My wife and I spent some days with him and his wife Ela (Hashi). They were an abstemious couple. He did not smoke or drink. We had to extort our quota of Scotch from him every evening. He was also very prudish. No talk of nudity or sex. No dirty jokes.

The air operations in the 1971 war against Pakistan were masterminded by Lal. It was his strategy that knocked out the teeth of the Pakistani Air Force in Bangladesh. Within a few hours of the declaration of the war, the Dacca and Chittagong airstrips were rendered unserviceable; the Pakistani Air Force mess next to the Dacca airport was knocked out by a direct hit and the Governor cowed to submission by a hail of bullets fired into the windows of his residence. Another trait that none of his contemporaries had suspected in Lal was efficiency and hard work. The way he streamlined the functioning of Air India and Indian Airlines, refusing doggedly to give in to arm-twisting by the pilots' union, earned him a deserved reputation as a first-class administrator.

Lal was a magnanimous man. He was removed from his post of Chairman of Air India and Indian Airlines by Sanjay Gandhi and took a job with the Tatas. When Sanjay fell from power and most people avoided meeting members of the Gandhi family, I had to go to Calcutta to appear as a co-accused with Maneka Gandhi in a case against *Surya*. I was staying with the Lals; Maneka with Kamal Nath.

'The Lals must hate us,' I recall Maneka telling me. Lal hated no one. It was Hashi who invited Maneka over to their house and instead of showing any resentment against what had been done to them, treated her with great courtesy and affection.

Pratap died in London on 13 August 1982. I was present at his cremation the next day in the Delhi electric crematorium. So ended a friendship that had lasted over half a century. Shakespeare's lines from *Julius Caesar* are the most fitting tribute I could pay to my departed friend:

> His life was gentle.
> And the elements so mixed in him
> That nature itself would stand up and say
> to all the world: This was a Man.

MANZUR QADIR
(1913–1974)

My closest friend of many years lay dying; I could not go to his bedside. His wife and children were only an hour-and-a-half's flight from me; I could not go to see them. I could not ring them up nor write to them. And when he died, I was not there to comfort them. They are Pakistani, I am Indian. What kind of neighbours are we? What right have we to call ourselves civilized?

I had missed the news in the morning paper. When a friend rang me up and said, 'Your old friend is gone,' the blood in my veins froze. I picked up the paper from the wastepaper basket and saw it in black and white. Manzur Qadir was dead. At the time he was dying in London, I was drinking and listening to Vividh Bharati in Bombay. And when he was being laid to rest in the family graveyard at Lahore, I was wringing my hands in despair in Colaba. He was Pakistani, I am Indian.

It is believed that when a person is dying, all the events of his life flash before his mind's eye. I must have occupied many precious seconds of Manzur Qadir's dying thoughts as he also regarded me as his closest friend. I spent the whole morning thinking of how we met and why I was drawn close to him. At our first meeting thirty years ago we had talked about death. I had quoted lines from the last letter his wife Asghari's brother had written to his father, Mian Fazl-i-Husain:

> I am working by candlelight,
> It flickers, it's gone.

Manzur Qadir was a man of contradictions. He showed little promise as a student; he became the most outstanding lawyer of Pakistan. Next to law, his favourite reading was the Old Testament and the Quran. Nevertheless he remained an agnostic to the very last. He was an uncommonly good poet and wrote some of the wittiest, bawdiest verse known in the Urdu language. At the same time he was extremely conservative, correct in his speech and deportment. Although born a Punjabi he rarely spoke the language and preferred to converse in Hindustani, which he did with uncommon elegance. He was long-winded but never a bore; a teetotaller who effervesced like vintage champagne.

The dominant traits of his character were kindliness—he never said a hurtful word about anyone—and integrity which surpassed belief. He made upwards of ₹50,000 a month; income tax authorities were constantly refunding tax he had paid in excess. He did not give a tinker's cuss about money. It was commonly said, 'God may lie, but not Manzur Qadir.' Though godless he had more goodness in him than a clutch of saints.

The respect and admiration he commanded among his friends was unparalleled. Some years after Partition, a group of us were discussing G. D. Khosla's *Stern Reckoning*. The book, as the title signifies, justified the killings that took place in East Punjab in the wake of Partition as legitimate retribution. We were going for Khosla's partisan approach; he and his wife were arguing back. Suddenly a friend asked Khosla, 'Would you present a copy of this book to Manzur?' Khosla pondered for a while and replied, 'No, not to him.' That ended the argument. We came to judge the right or wrong of our actions by how Manzur Qadir would react. He was the human touchstone of our moral pretensions.

Manzur Qadir had no interest in politics and seldom bothered to read newspapers. His ignorance of world affairs was abysmal. Once in London we happened to see a newsreel of Dr Sun Yat Sen. He asked me who this Sen was. When I expressed my amazement at his lack of information, he retorted testily: 'Hoga koee sala Bangali daktar.' Later in the evening, when I narrated the incident to his daughter Shireen, she chided her father. He made me swear I wouldn't tell anyone about it. I didn't till I read in the papers that President Ayub Khan had made him foreign minister of Pakistan. I sent him a telegram of congratulations, 'Greetings from Dr Sun Yat Sen, the Bengali doctor.'

I spent a short holiday with him when he was foreign minister. I stayed as a guest in my own home. (I had put him in possession of it when I left Lahore in August 1947. He not only saved the life of my Sikh servants, whom he brought to the Indian border at night at considerable risk to his life, but sent back every book in my library, every item of furniture and even the remaining liquor in my drinks cabinet.) He told me how he had become foreign minister. He had criticized Ayub Khan's dictatorship at a meeting. That evening an army jeep came to fetch him. Believing that he was being arrested he said goodbye to his family. He was driven to the President's residence.

Said Ayub Khan: 'It is no good criticizing me and my government unless you are willing to take responsibility for what you say.' Manzur Qadir returned home as foreign minister.

True to his character, Manzur never canvassed for any job nor showed the slightest eagerness to hold on to power. He strove with none, for none was worth his strife. He allowed himself to be outmanoeuvred by unscrupulous politicians. After four years as foreign minister, during which he made a desperate bid to improve relations with India, he quit the job with no regrets. He was forced to become chief justice and, when he desired to throw that up, persuaded to take up briefs on behalf of the government. He was engaged as government counsel in all the important conspiracy cases and represented his country before international tribunals; whether it was Iskander Mirza or Ayub Khan, Yahya Khan or Bhutto, no ruler of Pakistan could do without Manzur Qadir.

Last year I spent a day with him in Nathiagali near Murree. He was a very sick man afflicted with phlebitis. But for old times' sake, he drove down to Islamabad to pick me up and drove me back the next evening. I saw for myself the affection and esteem with which he was held by everyone from General Tikka Khan down to the humblest tradesman in the bazaar. It was a continuous shaking of hands and salaam alaikums.

He bore the pain of his illness with incredible courage and without the slightest attempt to find false props offered by religion. He knew he had a short time to go but had no fear of death. I forget the Urdu couplet he used to quote but it was very much like Charles Wesley's lines:

> If I must die, I will encounter darkness as a bride and hug it in my arms.

> When summoned hence to thine eternal sleep, oh, mayest
> thou smile while all round thee weep.

At our final farewell, the tears were in my eyes, not in his.

An English friend kept me informed of his deteriorating state of health in the London hospital. Apparently, she too was not with him when the end came. Tributes to such a man as Manzur Qadir can only be written in tears which leave no stain on paper. He shall be forever honoured and forever mourned. Robert Browning's lines were meant for a man like him:

> We that had loved him so, followed him, honoured him,
> Lived in his mild and magnificent eye,
> Learned his great language, caught his clear accents,
> Made him our pattern to live and to die.

Manzur Qadir died on 12 October 1974.

Whenever I visit Lahore, one of my top assignments is to visit his grave, strew rose petals on it, recite the fateha and shed some tears.

Basharat had chosen Allama Iqbal's lines for his father's epitaph:

> *Main to jaltee hoon ke muzmir meyree fitrat main soze*
> *Too ferozaan hai keh parvano se ho sanda teyra.*

> I burn because it is in my nature to do so
> Moths are drawn to you because with warmth you glow.

OTHERS

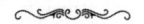

HARDAYAL
(1884-1939)

While I was still at school, the one name that was on all lips as the paradigm of the ultimate in scholarship was that of Hardayal. His name was always prefixed by two words—the great: he was the great Hardayal. Stories of his greatness as a student multiplied. He had a phenomenal memory: he only had to read a book once and he could reproduce its contents word for word; he was not only a topper in every subject, but he also broke previous records with wide margins in every exam he took.

Though this was not absolutely correct, because at times he was beaten by other examinees to the second place, people refused to believe it. What made his reputation impregnable was the fact that he was also a revolutionary who spurned government patronage, directed the Ghadar Movement in its early years in the US and Canada, became the principal adviser of the German government's attempt to foment a revolt against the British Raj during World War I.

Then, like his equally distinguished contemporary Veer Savarkar, he took a complete somersault, apologized for his past errors and pledged loyalty to them. One may well ask, if Veer Savarkar's portrait can be hung in our Parliament, why not Hardayal's?

Hardayal was born in Delhi on 4 October 1884, the sixth of seven children of Bhoti and Gauri Dayal Mathur, Reader of the District Court. He went to Cambridge Mission School and graduated from St. Stephen's College. He won a stipend and joined Government College, Lahore. He took his MA in English language and literature and another MA in history, breaking the university record for the highest marks. He won a scholarship to St. John's College, Oxford. While in India, he had been impressed by the Christian missionaries' selfless dedication and the Arya and Brahmo Samaj's attempts to purify Hinduism of meaningless rituals and superstition. He admired Lala Lajpat Rai and befriended Bhai Parmanand.

Hardayal joined Oxford University in 1905. He was twenty-one and married. He could have easily walked into any government job but had by now been infected by the bug of patriotism. 'To hell with the ICS,' he said, and refused to take the examination. He got to know Dadabhai Naoroji and Shyamaji Krishna Verma and decided to throw his lot in with the freedom struggle. He returned the stipend money to the government and quit Oxford.

He was somewhat of an ascetic. He never drank or smoked. He turned vegetarian, shed European clothes and took to wearing kurta and dhoti. He always slept on the floor.

He studied different religions and regarded the Buddha as his role model. He discussed the possibility of starting a new religion with Bhai Parmanand, who dissuaded him from doing so, saying, 'My own view is that all religions are a kind of fraud on mankind. You will be merely adding one more fraud.'

Hardayal made a meagre living by delivering lectures on Indian philosophy and writing articles. He edited Madam Cama's *Bande Mataram* and *Madan's Talwar*. In 1911, he went to America to study Buddhism at Harvard. Stanford University invited him to teach Indian philosophy. His radical views—he advocated free love—ended his tenure at Stanford. He had also taken up with a Swiss girl, Fried Hauswirth, which scandalized his American and Indian admirers. While still at Stanford, Hardayal made contacts with Indian workers in the West Coast and went across to help them organize the Ghadar Party. When they got news of the attempt to kill Viceroy Hardinge on 23 December 1912 in Delhi, Hardayal was among other Indians at Berkeley to celebrate the occasion, doing bhangra and singing 'Bande Mataram'.

The Ghadar Party was formed on 1 November 1913, with Hardayal as its guiding spirit. He was arrested by the US police and on release decided to go to Switzerland to rejoin Fried Hauswirth. In turn she came to the US to formalize her divorce and instead of joining Hardayal, married another Indian, Sarangdhar Das.

World War I broke out on 4 August 1914. Hardayal spent the early years of the war in Germany and Turkey, planning an invasion of India by a liberation force. He was naive enough to believe that the

Germans were eager to see India a free country. It took him a long time to see through the subterfuge and he turned into a bitter critic of the Germans and Turks. Of the latter, he opined: 'Turks have no brains...as a nation they are utterly unfit to assume the leadership of the Muslim world.' Of the Germans, who had financed his ventures, he wrote that they were 'without character...avaricious. They work hard and are patriotic but that is perhaps their only virtue.' He became an ardent admirer of the British as a 'truthful people...who had a moral and historical mission in India'. The British government had his pronouncements translated into Hindi and distributed free in India.

Hardayal had nowhere to go except to a neutral country. He chose Sweden. He had taken up with a Swedish woman, Agda Erikson, and with some difficulty managed to get a Swedish visa. He spent many years in Sweden, learned to speak Swedish and thirteen other languages. He lived with Agda, who described herself as Mrs Hardayal. He wrote several books of which *Hints on Self Culture* is the best known and sells to this day. He was allowed to return to England and was finally granted amnesty by the British with permission to go back to India. He was never able to do so. While on a lecture tour of the US, he died in his sleep in Philadelphia on 4 March 1939.

He was only fifty-four.

A heart-broken Agda Erikson took his ashes back to her native Sweden. That was all the great Hardayal left for her. His worldly wealth, for what it was worth, he left to his wife and daughter, Shanti, whom he never saw.

J. R. D. TATA
(1904-1993)

India owes more to the house of Tata than to any other industrial family for putting it on the path of self-sufficiency in areas vital for its survival in the modern world. They were pioneers in many fields, from the production of steel, hydel power, airlines, automobiles and nuclear research, down to the production of cosmetics and tea. And in every undertaking they strove to make their products as good, if not better, than those of their rivals. Along with these money-making enterprises, they built hospitals, educational institutions and extended patronage to the arts. More significantly, while other industrial houses were not averse to kowtowing to ministers and civil servants to get their deals through, the Tatas maintained high standards of rectitude (unique to Parsi industrialists and professionals), untainted by personal greed. Till recent years, the Tata board of management was entirely Parsi.

The Tata success story began when Jamsetji Tata set up a company to mine coal and iron ore in Bihar. In the years to come, it became India's largest steel production centre; the city that grew around it was renamed Jamshedpur. The real diversification and spectacular upsurge in the Tatas' fortunes came during J. R. D.'s fifty-two-year tenure at the helm of its affairs. He took over as chairman at the age of thirty-four and guided its course till he died in 1993.

Jehangir Tata (Jeh to his friends) was born in Paris. His father was Parsi, his mother, French. He spent the better part of his younger days in Paris, and French was his mother tongue. He was sent to a grammar school in England for two years. Being hard-working and studious, he picked up English and began to speak it as fluently as French. He was anxious to join Cambridge but his father summoned him to Bombay to join the family business. He developed a chip on his shoulder for never having gone to university. Bombay was his home for the rest of his life. Though he frequently asserted that he was an Indian (many Parsis do so grudgingly), neither his biography nor his letters reveal whether or not he could speak Gujarati or any other Indian language.

How much of a Parsi was he? In a letter, J. R. D. wrote: 'I am anything but a good Zoroastrian, at least in the sense of being a practicing one.' I'm not sure if he ever went inside an agiary—the Parsi fire temple.

J. R. D. was unabashed about the positive role of capitalism in a developing country. The word had become synonymous with 'bloodsuckers of the poor'. He took up cudgels on its behalf against the half-baked socialism preached by Nehru and JP.

Flying and fast cars were his abiding passions. He was the first Indian to get a pilot's licence and competed in the Aga Khan Trophy for the fastest flight from London to India. He was beaten to second place by another Parsi, Aspy Engineer (later Air Chief Marshal of the Indian Air Force). He knew every new kind of airplane from two-seaters to jumbo jets. It was the same with racing cars, his favourite being a Bugatti.

J. R. D. had a very sharp eye for detail. Every time he travelled on his own Air India planes, he put down his suggestions: why did the coffee and tea taste the same? Why two paper bags of sugar with each cup? Why were the omelettes leathery? When staying in one of the Taj Hotels, he noted that one large double bed disturbed the sleep of elderly couples; telephones in the bedroom and the bathroom should have separate numbers. When sent a sample of Lakmé products, he tried out every item from shaving creams, deodorants and colognes and compared them with the best products abroad. Once, while visiting Rashtrapati Bhavan, he noticed a gaffe under the portrait of the president. It read 'President swearing at ceremony'. He wrote to Babu Rajendra Prasad informing him of the difference between swearing in and swearing at.

J. R. D. led a full life and departed without any regrets. The last words he spoke were in French: 'I am about to discover a new world. It is going to be very interesting.' He's been gone for many years but his footprints will remain indelibly printed on the sands of time.

G. D. BIRLA
(1894–1983)

If a list of the builders of modern India were to be drawn up, the Birlas would undoubtedly be on top. There is, of course, the house of Tata but they kept themselves aloof from politics, politicians and the media. The Birlas, on the other hand, took a keen interest in political affairs, financed political parties and politicians and published newspapers. As a result, they were always in the public eye. They were also the biggest builders of temples in modern times, earning respect in every Hindu house.

The most famous among the Birlas was Ghanshyam Das. The Birlas are Marwaris from Pilani and belong to the Maheswari subcaste. Strict vegetarians and teetotallers, they venerate the cow and conform to Vaishnavite rituals. They marry within their subcaste: a breach of this tradition can invite ostracism. For years they regarded the crossing of the seas as sinful and had to undergo ritual cleansing before being readmitted. They prospered as small-time traders in Pilani till they found greener pastures in the metros, mainly Bombay and Calcutta. Wherever they went, they carried their family traditions with them and remained a close-knit community. They earned goodwill where they settled by generous donations to charitable institutions.

By the time G. D. was brought to Calcutta in the 1890s, the family was well set on the road to opulence: his father, Baldev Das, had acquired the honorific of raja. They made their home in the Marwari mohalla of Bara Bazaar. Fortunes were built on trading in opium, import of cloth and jute. For a while, G. D. was sent to Bombay where he picked up English and read the classics. He followed the strict regimen of his childhood, rising well before dawn and spending at least two hours before sunrise in prayer and physical exercise. (He even toyed with the idea of becoming a professional wrestler.) Back in Calcutta, he joined the Bengali terrorists. He was named among those wanted in the Rodda conspiracy case to smuggle arms and went underground for three months.

There was an upward swing in the Birlas' fortunes in 1911. Besides opium and silver, they made a killing supplying jute bags and uniforms to the army when World War I broke out. They went into the textile industry in a big way, setting up mills across the country. They also acquired two English newspapers, the *New Empire* and *Bengalee*. G. D. also became the chief spokesman of the Marwari community in the European-dominated Chambers of Commerce and the Bengal assembly. He was always involved in politics. His instinctive bias was towards right-wing Hindu nationalism and he generously gave money to Pandit Madan Mohan Malviya and the Banares Hindu University. He was also taken with Lala Lajpat Rai—he gave him money for personal expenses—and his Servants of India society. Ultimately Birla turned to Mahatma Gandhi, extended him hospitality in the Birla houses in Calcutta, Bombay and Delhi, and bailed out the Congress when it was in dire need of funds. It was no coincidence that the Mahatma was staying at Birla House in Delhi when his assassins got him. The Birlas donated the house to the nation.

G. D. was never one to take the steering wheel but was content to remain a backseat driver. But with the Mahatma's death, he lost this privileged position. For a while, Pandit Nehru heeded his advice. Birla approved of the first five-year plan setting out the roles of the public and private sectors in nation building. As Nehru decided to keep his distance from big business houses, and put his idea of socialism into practice, the Birlas receded into the background. Birla disapproved of the second five-year plan and the influence of P. C. Mahalanobis in decision-making. Birla tried to re-establish contact with the government when Indira Gandhi became prime minister. But she inherited her father's distrust of industrialists. 'Our private enterprise is more private than enterprising,' she scoffed. She returned a gift he had sent on Rajiv's marriage. But she accepted his money. Likewise, Morarji Desai disdained associating with him but had no compunction taking money from him. G. D. abandoned his attempts to influence the government and contented himself with his business enterprises and his extended family. His health began to fail. He died in London on 11 June 1983 and according to his wishes was cremated there. His sons brought his ashes to India to be immersed in the Ganga.

NARGIS DUTT
(1929–1981)

For many years, the picture of Nargis troubled my midnights, and my noon reposes. She remained a lovely, distant apparition beyond the approach of earthly mortals like me. Then one morning my telephone rang and a dulcet voice announced:

'This is Nargis Dutt speaking. Can I speak to Mr So-&-so?'

'It is So-&-so speaking. Would you by any means be Nargis the film star?'

'Ji-haan.'

'Mother India and all that?'

'Ji-haan. Can I come and see you?'

An hour later, she breezed into my office setting many a heart wildly aflutter. She was as beautiful as she was unassuming and friendly. 'I have come to ask you for a personal favour,' she said. 'I believe you have a house in Kasauli. My children are at Sanawar and I can't find anywhere to stay during the school Founder's Week celebrations. I was wondering if you could let me stay in your house.'

'Of course!' I replied. 'But only on one condition.' I paused to create the necessary suspense. She looked quizzically at me:

'What?'

'Provided thereafter I have your permission to tell anyone I like that Nargis slept in my bed.'

Nargis repeated this dialogue many times without the slightest embarrassment. She had the knack of making people happy. And a malicious sense of humour. But the last time she was in Delhi to attend the session of the Rajya Sabha, she was somewhat lacking in her usual exuberance. 'I shouldn't be here. My doctor told me I have some kind of jaundice. I promised the local Rotary I would come—I couldn't break my word, could I? And there is this debate on Baghpat.'

The debate, as you might recall, was largely the tirade let loose by the Opposition on the shooting of three men and the alleged rape of

Maya Tyagi in the police station. The atmosphere in the House was charged with emotion. A lady member, somewhat dark and corpulent, exploded a volcano of angry epithets, pouring lava on the government which though headed by a woman allowed women to be insulted, molested and raped. 'There is a rape here and a rape there! Every day we hear of rape, rape, rape,' she shrilled. Nargis who was sitting next to me became suddenly very animated. 'Why are you getting so excited?' she shouted. 'No one will ever rape you.' Mercifully, only a few members sitting near her heard her remark and laughed jovially.

Nargis was very sick. In New York, the receptionist at the Memorial Sloan Kettering Hospital was not impressed by my telling her that I had come across half the world to see her. 'Are you her husband?' she demanded, somewhat exasperated at my insistence.

'Alas no,' I replied, 'only a distant friend and an ardent admirer.'

So Nargis is gone. I for one had never believed that she had been discharged from Sloan Kettering as cured; they were of the opinion that nothing more could be done for her and she decided to come home to die.

Now boast thee, death, in thy possession lies
A lass unparalleled.

Beautiful she was in all senses of the word. Shaped in the classic mould, enshrining a heart of gold which went out to the poor, the blind and the paraplegic. Her smile was bewitching, her laughter contagious. She had the gift of eternal youth and died looking as young in her fifties as she had been in her teens.

One thing that intrigued me was her faith. Was she Muslim or Hindu or both or nothing? She wore a bindi on her forehead, married a Brahmin, gave her children Hindu names and was often seen in Swami Mutkananda's ashram at Ganeshpuri. Nevertheless, she was buried with Muslim rites in a Muslim graveyard with her Hindu husband reciting the fateha (prayer). I can't think of any Indian family which better exemplified the principle of Sarva Dharma Samabhav (equal respect for all faiths).

My chief claim to fame as a Member of the Rajya Sabha was that I sat next to Nargis and was the envy of my brother parliamentarians. That seat has remained unoccupied since last August. No doubt someone else will be nominated to fill her place. But the void she leaves in the hearts of millions of her countrymen will never be filled.

PROTIMA BEDI
(1949–1998)

Protima Gupta was born in Delhi in 1949. Her father, a small-time trader, was thrown out by his Bania father for marrying a dark Bengali woman. He tried his luck in different cities of India, flopped everywhere and rejoined his family business. They had four children: three daughters and a son. Protima was their second daughter and the least loved. A loveless childhood turned her into a rebel. She was a bright girl and did well in her studies. Two words that were missing in her life's lexicon were 'no' and 'regret'; she could not say no to any man who desired her—and grew into a very desirable and highly animated young woman whom most men found irresistible. And she did not regret any emotional or physical experience she had. She also felt that keeping secrets was like lying; so she told everyone everything, including her husband and the succession of lovers who entered her life. She broke up marriages and remained blissfully unaware of the hurt she caused people. She had to get everything off her chest. She told nothing but the truth about everyone she befriended. She might have added a few more chapters to her life story: why she abandoned her dance school and other business to become a sanyasin, but death took her unawares—she was killed in a landslide while on a pilgrimage to Kailash-Manasarovar on 18 August 1998. Oddly enough, even as a sanyasin, she was accompanied by one of her lovers. And on the same day in Bombay died Persis Khambatta, India's first beauty queen and one-time mistress of Protima's husband, Kabir Bedi.

I first met Protima in the home of Gopi Gauba in Bombay. Kabir, whom I had known as a child in Lahore, was with her. I had little reason to like them as he had just ditched my friend B. G. Sanyal's daughter, Amba, to whom he was engaged and was living with Protima who was then only nineteen years old. I did not exchange a word with either of them. When Protima became pregnant, they decided to get married. Pooja was their first child. But neither marriage nor having a child made either Protima or Kabir change their ways. While Kabir was away shooting some film with some starlet to keep him happy, Protima, mother of eight-month-old Pooja, was having an affair with a young German living next door. She was not sure if her son Siddhartha was from her husband or her pro-tem lover. She confessed her doubts to her husband and later told her son. The boy became a schizophrenic and later committed suicide in the USA.

Next I saw photographs of Protima running stark naked on a beach in Goa. It shocked middle-class society—exactly what she wanted to do. One day, when I was editing the *Illustrated Weekly of India*, I. S. Jauhar asked me to come over with a photographer as he was getting engaged to Protima. On the phone I called him an ass but I went. I published their photograph exchanging rings. That's all they wanted: publicity. Protima later assured me that she had not as much as kissed Jauhar. I believed her because Protima never lied.

I did not see Protima blossom into an Odissi dancer. Nor did I see the dance village Nrityagram which she had created. She came to Bangalore to invite me. I accepted the invitation but when I discovered it would take me four hours on the road to get there and back, I called it off. She was very angry with me and swore she would never see me again. Her anger did not last long. When her son took his own life, she shaved off her long hair and renounced worldly pursuits. On her return to India she asked me to let her stay in my villa in Kasauli for a few days to be near Sanawar where her son had been at school for a short time. She spent four cold winter days walking about the hills all alone. She returned refreshed and full of smiles. Protima Gauri (as she renamed herself) had a zest for living.

She loved her men, her liquor and drugs. She had a large range of lovers, most of whom she named. They include the singer Pandit Jasraj and the late Rajni Patel with whom she exchanged love letters till he was hospitalized and his wife Bakul forbade communication between them. Among the last was a businessman who abandoned his family and business to serve her.

It must have taken a lot of courage for her daughter Pooja to edit her mother's memoirs and decide to have them published. 'Passion, compassion and laughter,' writes Pooja, were the three words which summed up her mother's personality in *Timepass: The Memoirs of Protima Bedi*. Protima hated humbugs and hypocrites. She wrote, 'Every woman I knew secretly longed to have many lovers but she stopped herself for so many reasons. I had the capacity to love many at a time and for this had been called shallow and wayward and a good-time girl...'

I bless Protima for being the kind of person she was. I bless Pooja for letting us know what her mother had to say about herself. Many readers may be shocked at the revelations, many of her lovers who are still living and their wives and children will be acutely embarrassed by her disclosures but no one will be able to put down *Timepass* once he or she starts reading it.

CHETAN ANAND
(1921–1997)

For many years we were the closest of friends. Our jobs took us to distant cities. Nevertheless, we remained in constant touch. The closeness lasted for over thirty years. Then he turned indifferent and I felt hurt. He was one of the people I wrote about in my *Women and Men in My Life*. He was hurt by what I had to say about him. That had not been my intention. Nevertheless, when I heard of his death on the morning of Sunday, 6 July 1997, I was overcome with remorse and sorrow.

Our past association haunted me for several days and nights. Our friendship began in 1932 when we found ourselves in the same class in Government College, Lahore, studying the same subjects and living in the same hostel. Chetan was a very pretty boy: fair, with curly hair and dreamy eyes.

He started seeking my company more to protect himself, and not so much because he shared common interests with me. We ate our breakfasts together, attended classes together, played tennis in the afternoons and, at least twice a week, went to the movies. During vacations he went home to Gurdaspur. We wrote to each other. He was into writing poetry à la Gurudev Tagore. He sent his compositions to me. Soppy stuff, but I was flattered.

Chetan had to count his rupees. One year he put himself up for election for the secretaryship of the Hindu-Sikh dining room, and, as was the custom those days, had cards printed soliciting votes. I could not understand why anyone would want to oversee cooking and feeding arrangements in a college hostel mess. I discovered that catering contractors bestowed extra favours to secretaries by not charging them for meals. The elections were as fiercely contested as those of the college union. Chetan won.

After we passed out of college, we found ourselves together in London. I was studying law; he came to take a shot at the ICS. We both took the examination. Neither of us made the grade. Chetan could not afford to stay on in England and returned home.

We resumed our friendship when I came back to Delhi. He and Iqbal Singh were the only two friends I invited to my wedding in October 1939. A year later, when I set up practice in Lahore, Chetan spent many months of the summer in my flat. Though till then he had not found a job, he was highly successful in winning the favours of young ladies. His technique was simple. On hot June afternoons, he would go in his overcoat carrying a single rose in his hand. When the recipient of the rose asked him why he was wearing an overcoat, he would answer, 'Because it is the only thing I possess in the world.'

One who fell heavily for this approach was the ravishing Uma, daughter of Professor Chatterjee. We celebrated their engagement in my apartment. That very evening I caught him flirting with another girl. He was never a one-woman man. Uma married him, had two sons and then left him to become Ebrahim Alkazi's second wife. Chetan shifted to Bombay to try his luck in films. There he shacked up with Priya, who was a good twenty years younger than him. He did his best to turn her into a film star. He did not succeed.

Chetan did not make his mark as a director or an actor as his obituaries now claim. He made one good film, *Neecha Nagar*; the rest were second-rate, and earned him neither fame nor money. He did an excellent job reproducing the light and sound show at the Red Fort in Delhi for which I had written the master script in 1965. He got assignments from the Punjab government which he was unable to fulfil.

It was not his successes or failures in films that affected my affection for him; it was his indifference towards me when I moved to Bombay to take up the editorship of the *Illustrated Weekly of India* in 1969. I was there for a whole nine years and expected to see a lot of Chetan. I saw something of my other college friends: Balraj Sahni, B. R. Chopra, Kamini Kaushal and even Chetan's brother, Dev Anand. But Chetan, with whom I looked forward to resuming my close friendship, did not bother to contact me even once. Only a month or so before I left Bombay I ran into him and his lady friend at a party. Very airily he said, 'Oi Sardar! Tu milta hee nahin. (O Sardar! You never meet me.)' I exploded with anger, 'Besharam! You shameless creature! Is this the way you fulfil the obligations of a forty-year-old friendship?'

His lady friend tried to protest and invited me to come over. 'I don't want to set foot in your home or see this fellow's face again,' I replied and stormed out.

Now I regret what I said as I recall Chetan with tears in my eyes.

RANJIT SINGH
(1780–1839)

Maharaja Ranjit Singh was undoubtedly the greatest son of the Punjab, but he was not a handsome, anaemic, saintly character. He was a small, ugly man who loved the good things in life, liquor, good-looking men and women around him. He loved horses and leading his troops in battle. To wit Rudyard Kipling:

> Four things greater than all things are
> Women and horses and power and War.

While still a boy, Ranjit got smallpox, which blinded him in one eye and left his face pockmarked. Emily Eden, who was with her brother the Governor General, Lord Auckland, when they called on the maharaja, described him as 'exactly like an old mouse, with grey whiskers, one eye and a grey beard'. A legend claims that his favourite Muslim mistress, Bibi Mohran, in whose name he had a coin struck, once asked him where he was when God was distributing good looks. He replied, 'When you were asking for a comely appearance, I asked Him for power.' Before meeting him, the Governor General asked the maharaja's chief minister, Fakir Azizuddin, what his master looked like. Fakir Azizuddin gave him a diplomatic answer: 'His face has so much jalaal (dazzle) that I have never dared to look at him.'

Emily Eden wrote about Ranjit Singh's partiality for strong liquor. Dr Martin Honigberger, who prepared gunpowder for the maharaja's artillery, also prepared brandy for the royal table.

At the state banquet, Emily took care to sit on the blind-eye side of the maharaja, who poured the drinks himself in the gold goblets of the guests seated on either side of him. Every time he turned to talk to the Governor General, Emily quietly emptied her goblet on the carpet. Ranjit filled it over and over again and then turned to one of his courtiers and said in Punjabi: 'Mem taan khoob peendee hai (this white woman can hold her drink).' Once he asked a Frenchman whether it was better for the health to drink after a meal as some doctors advised or before the meal as others said. The Frenchman replied that drinking, both before and after meals, was good for one's health. The maharaja roared with happy laughter.

One aspect of Ranjit Singh's character, which made him unique among the Indian rulers, was that he was totally free of religious prejudice. Though slaughter of kine was forbidden and many of his Hindu and European officers did not cut their hair and beards to please him, he did not impose his views on anyone. His council of ministers was dominated by the three Fakir brothers; it included Dogras and, of course, Sardars, Sandhawalias, Majithas, Attariwalas and others. Likewise, his army, trained by European officers, comprised all communities. The cavalry was largely Sikh, the artillery, commanded by General Elahi Bakhsh, largely Muslim, and the infantry, a mix of Dogras, Gorkhas, Sikhs and Muslim Najibs. His commanders on the battlefield were men like Diwan Mohkam Chand and his son, Diwan Chand, Hari Singh Nalwa and Prince Sher Singh. In short, it was a composite Punjabi fighting force that created history by reversing the tide of conquests back to the homelands of the traditional invaders—the Pathans and the Afghans.

Nothing proves Ranjit's credentials more than when it came to determining the future of the diamond, Kohinoor. Instead of leaving it to one of his sons or donating it to the Harmandir, which he had renovated in marble and gold leaf, he wished it to be given to the temple of Jagannath in Puri.

It is ironic that it was the Akali Dal-BJP government of Punjab, led by Prakash Singh Badal, that took the lead in organizing the celebrations of the second centenary of his coronation some years ago. Ranjit Singh had little respect for the Akalis of his time: 'Kuj faham wa kotch andesh (of crooked minds and short-sightedness).'

On my way back from an interview, which took place in Metcalfe House, I happened to pass through Sabzi Mandi. The street was blocked by what seemed to be some kind of fracas taking place ahead. I asked the driver to stop and went out to find out what it was. 'We've caught a couple of Muslim swine trying to take a cow for slaughter,' someone from the crowd informed me. I pushed my way through the mob and came to the centre of the scene. There was a cow and three men—two Muslims and a Sikh—surrounded by men armed with steel rods and long knives. My arrival, clad in suit and tie, deterred them. 'What's going on?' I demanded angrily. 'These two fellows are butchers; this Sikh sold the cow to them,' I was informed. All three men were shaking with fear. The Muslims had been stripped naked and seen to be circumcised. The Sikh was to be beaten up and taught a lesson. I put my arms in front of the butchers and shouted back, 'No one is going to touch these men! I have seen enough of this during Partition. It has to stop.'

The crowd turned nasty towards me. 'Do you understand that these men were going to butcher this cow? What kind of a Sikh are you?' I held my ground. 'I will not let you touch them. If anyone does, I'll have him arrested. I am a government official.' They were not impressed. But no one was willing to make the first move. I thought of a way out. 'Let's take them to the police station and see what we can do.' The crowd let me do what I wanted. I led the cow, and put my arms around the two butchers; the bloodthirsty mob followed in trams clanking madly at us to clear the way. We arrived at the Sabzi Mandi police station. I introduced myself to the inspector in charge, a Punjabi Hindu, and pleaded with him to take the butchers into custody. The Sikh had meanwhile slipped away into the crowd. 'They have committed no crime, why should I arrest them?' he demanded. 'To save their lives,' I pleaded. He was adamant. I threatened him with my status as an official. He could not care less. 'I don't care who you are or what the crowd will do to these fellows. They deserve what is coming to them.'

I resumed my march with the cow and the butchers through the crowded bazaar to Tis Hazari where there was a veterinary hospital. By the time I got there, the crowd had thinned. The vet was a white-bearded Sikh. I pleaded with him to take the cow into custody and to arrest the two men on the charge of cruelty to animals. He was adamant. 'I see no injury on the cow. And if they want to kill these snakes I am not going to stop them,' he said, walking away. I turned to address the few would-be killers who remained. 'Look, I will release the cow here and now and take these fellows to some place where I can teach them the lesson they deserve.' They agreed, they had had enough, their tempers had cooled. I let the cow loose. It ran across the open ground with its tail raised, kicking its hind legs in the sheer joy of being released from human bondage. I ordered the two butchers to get into my car. 'Where do you live?' I asked them.

'Daryaganj.'

'Don't you fellows realize how dangerous it is in these times to slaughter kine?'

'Janab, we had nothing to eat for two days. We pooled our resources to buy this cow. Now we are ruined.'

I dropped them at Daryaganj. They did not go to their homes. I saw them turn back to go and look for the cow they had bought.

I am not a brave man. I was amazed at the audacity I had shown in the face of danger. I asked the chauffeur to take me to Gurdwara Sisganj in Chandni Chowk. By now I had given up visiting places of worship. Sisganj marked the site of the execution of the ninth Guru, Tegh Bahadur. According to the legend, he had laid down his life to protect Hindus from persecution. It was the best place to go to for one who in his small way had saved the lives of two Muslims. At Sisganj I offered obeisance at the Guru's shrine, which is in an underground cell where the trunk of the banyan tree under which he was beheaded is preserved. I thanked the Guru for giving a coward like me the courage to uphold what I thought was a Sikh's duty. I broke down; tears of gratitude welled up in my eyes. As I left, my legs shook. I had come close to being murdered.

At home I narrated the incident with great pride. Far from being applauded I was called 'bewakoof' (a fool) and 'gadha' (a donkey) by my father's friend Sohan Singh of Rawalpindi who was staying with him. My mother was angry that I had put my life in jeopardy. My father kept silent. I knew I had the approval of the one man who mattered more to me than anyone else.

◆

POSTHUMOUS

I am in bed with fever. It is not serious. In fact, it is not serious at all, as I have been left alone to look after myself. I wonder what would happen if the temperature suddenly shot up. Perhaps I would die. That would be really hard on my friends. I have so many and am so popular. I wonder what the papers would have to say about it. They couldn't just ignore me. Perhaps *The Tribune* would mention it on its front page with a small photograph. The headline would read 'Sardar Khushwant Singh Dead'—and then in somewhat smaller print:

> We regret to announce the sudden death of Sardar Khushwant Singh at 6 p.m. last evening. He leaves behind a young widow, two infant children and a large number of friends and admirers to mourn his loss. It will be recalled that the Sardar came to settle in Lahore some five years ago from his hometown, Delhi. Within these years he rose to a position of eminence in the Bar and in politics. His loss will be mourned generally throughout the province.
>
> Among those who called at the late Sardar's residence were the PA to the prime minister, the PA to the chief justice, several ministers and judges of the high court.
>
> In a statement to the press, the hon'ble chief justice said: 'I feel that the Punjab is poorer by the passing away of this man. The cruel hand of death has cut short the promise of a brilliant career.'

At the bottom of the page would be an announcement:
The funeral will take place at 10 a.m. today.

I feel very sorry for myself and for all my friends. With difficulty I check the tears which want to express sorrow at my own death. But I also feel elated and want people to mourn me. So I decide to die—just for the fun of it as it were. In the evening, giving enough time for the press to hear of my death, I give up the ghost. Having emerged from my corpse, I come down and sit on the cool marble steps at the entrance to wallow in posthumous glory.

In the morning I get the paper before my wife. There is no chance of a squabble over the newspaper as I am downstairs already, and in any case my wife is busy pottering around my corpse. *The Tribune* lets me down. At the bottom of Page 3, Column 1, I find myself inserted in little brackets of obituary notices of retired civil servants—and that is all. I feel annoyed. It must be that blighter, Shafi, special representative. He never liked me. But I couldn't imagine he would be so mean as to deny me a little importance when I was dead. However, he couldn't keep the wave of sorrow which would run over the province from trickling into his paper. My friends would see to that.

Near the high court the paper is delivered fairly early. In the house of my lawyer friend, Qadir, it is deposited well before dawn. It isn't that the Qadirs are early risers. As a matter of fact, hardly anyone stirs in the house before 9 a.m. But Qadir is a great one for principles and he insists that the paper must be available early in the morning even if it is not looked at.

As usual, the Qadirs were in bed at 9 a.m. He had worked very late at night. She believed in sleep anyhow. The paper was brought in on a tray along with a tumbler of hot water with a dash of lime juice. Qadir sipped the hot water between intervals of cigarette smoking. He had to do this to make his bowels work. He only glanced at the headlines in bed. The real reading was done when the cigarette and lime had had their effect. The knowledge of how fate had treated me had to await the lavatory.

In due course, Qadir ambled into the bathroom with the paper in one hand and a cigarette perched on his lower lip. Comfortably seated, he began to scan it thoroughly and his eye fell on news of lesser import. When he got to Page 3, Column 1, he stopped smoking for a moment, a very brief moment. Should he get up and shout to his wife? No, he decided, that would be an unnecessary demonstration. Qadir was a rationalist. He had become more of one since he married a woman who was a bundle of emotions and explosions. The poor fellow was dead and nothing could be done about it. He knew that his wife would burst out crying when he told her. That was all the more reason that he should be matter-of-fact about it—just as if he was going to tell her of a case he had lost.

Qadir knew his wife well. He told her with an air of casualness, and she burst out crying. Her ten-year-old daughter came running into the room. She eyed her mother for a little while and then joined her in the wailing. Qadir decided to be severe.

'What are you making all this noise for?' he said sternly. 'Do you think it will bring him back to life?'

His wife knew that it was no use arguing with him. He always won the arguments.

'I think we should go to their house at once. His wife must be feeling wretched,' she said.

Qadir shrugged his shoulders.

'I am afraid I can't manage it. Much as I would like to condole with his wife—rather widow—my duty to my clients comes first. I have to be at the tribunal in half an hour.'

Qadir was at the tribunal all day and his family stopped at home.

Not far from the city's big park lives another friend, Khosla. He and his family, consisting of a wife, three sons and a daughter, reside in this upper-class residential area. He is a judge and very high up in the bureaucracy.

Khosla is an early riser. He has to rise early because that is the only time he has to himself. During the day he has to work in the courts. In the evenings he plays tennis—and then he has to spend some time with the children and fussing with his wife. He has a large number of visitors, as he is very popular and enjoys popularity. But Khosla is ambitious. As a lad he had fancied himself as a clever boy. In his early youth his hair had begun to fall off and had uncovered a large bald forehead. Khosla had looked upon it as nature's confirmation of his opinion about himself. Perhaps he was a genius. The more he gazed upon his large head in the mirror, the more he became convinced that fate had marked for him an extraordinary career. So he worked harder. He won scholarships and rounded off his academic career by topping the list in the civil service examination. He had justified the confidence he had in himself by winning laurels in the stiffest competitive examination in the country. For some years he lived the life of a contented bureaucrat. In fact, he assured himself that he was what people called 'a success in life'.

After some years this contentment had vanished. Every time he brushed the little tuft at the back of his head and ran his hands across his vast forehead he became conscious of unrealized expectations. There were hundreds of senior civil servants like him. All were considered successes in life. The civil service was obviously not enough. He would work—he would write—he knew he could write. There it was written in the size of his head. So Khosla took to writing. In order to write well he took to reading. He amassed a large library and regularly spent some hours in it before going to work.

This morning Khosla happened to be in a mood to write. He made himself a cup of tea and settled in a comfortable armchair by the electric radiator. He stuck the pencil in his mouth and meditated. He couldn't think of what to write. He decided to write his diary. He had spent the previous day listening to an important case. It was likely to go on for some days. The courtroom had been packed and everyone had been looking at him—that seemed a good enough subject. So he started to write.

Khosla was disturbed by the knock of the bearer bringing in the paper. He opened the news-sheet to read the truths of mundane existence.

Khosla was more interested in social affairs, births, marriages and deaths, than events of national or international import. He turned to Page 3, Column 1. His eye caught the announcement and he straightened up.

He just tapped his notebook with his pencil, and after a wake-up cough informed his wife of the news. She just yawned and opened her large, dreamy eyes wide.

'I suppose you will close the high court today?' she said.

'I am afraid the high court doesn't close at just any excuse. I'll have to go. If I have any time I'll drop in on the way—or we can call on Sunday.'

The Khoslas did not come. Nor did many others for whose sorrow at my demise I had already felt sorrowful.

At 10 o'clock a little crowd had collected in front of the open space beneath my flat. It consisted mainly of people I did not expect to see. There were some lawyers in their court dress, and a number of sightseers who wanted to find out what was happening. Two friends of mine also turned up, but they stood apart from the crowd. One was a tall, slim man who looked like an artist. With one hand he kept his cigarette in place, the other he constantly employed in pushing his long hair off his forehead. He was a writer. He did not believe in attending funerals. But one had to hang around for a little while as a sort of social obligation. It was distasteful to him. There was something infectious about a corpse—so he smoked incessantly and made a cigarette smokescreen between himself and the rest of the world.

The other friend was a communist, a short, slight man with wavy hair and a hawkish expression. His frame and expression belied the volcano that they camouflaged. His approach to everything was coldly Marxist and sentiment found no place in it. Deaths were unimportant events. It was the cause that mattered. He consulted the writer in a polite whisper.

'How far are you going?'

'I plan dropping off at the coffee house,' answered the other. 'Are you going the whole way?'

'No ruddy fear,' said the communist emphatically. 'Actually I had to be at a meeting at ten, and I was planning to be free of this by 9.30—but you know our people haven't the foggiest idea about time. I'll get along to the party office now and then meet you at the coffee house at 11.30. Incidentally, if you get the opportunity, just ask the hearse driver if he is a member of the Tongawala Union. Cheers.'

A little later, a hearse, drawn by a bony brown horse, pulled up in front of my doorstep. The horse and his master were completely oblivious to the solemnity of the occasion. The driver sat placidly chewing his betel nut and eyeing the assembly. He was wondering whether this was the type likely to produce a tip. The beast straightaway started to piddle and the crowd scattered to avoid the spray which rebounded off the brick floor.

The crowd did not have to wait very long. My corpse was brought down, all tied up in white linen, and placed inside the hearse. A few flowers were ceremoniously placed on me. The procession was ready to start.

Before we moved, another friend turned up on his bicycle. He was somewhat dark and flabby. He carried several books on the carrier and had the appearance of a scholarly, serious-minded professor. As soon as he saw the loaded hearse, he dismounted. He had great respect for the dead and was particular to express it. He put his bicycle in the hall, chained it, and joined the crowd. When my wife came down to bid her last farewell he was visibly moved. From his pocket he produced a little book and thoughtfully turned over its pages. Then he slipped through the people towards my wife. With tears in his eyes he handed the book to her.

'I've brought you a copy of the Gita. It will give you great comfort.' Overcome with emotion, he hurriedly slipped back to wipe the tears which had crept into his eyes.

'This,' he said to himself with a sigh, 'is the end of human existence. This is the truth.'

He was fond of thinking in platitudes—but to him all platitudes were profound and had the freshness and vigour of original thought.

'Like bubbles,' he said to himself, 'human life is as momentary as a bubble.'

But one didn't just die and disappear. Matter could not immaterialize—it could only change its form. The Gita put it so beautifully:

'Like a man casts off old garments to put on new ones...so does the soul, etc., etc.'

The professor was lost in contemplation. He wondered what new garments his dead friend had donned.

His thoughts were disturbed by a movement between his legs. A little pup came round the professor's legs, licking his trousers and looking up at him. The professor was a kind man. He involuntarily bent down and patted the little dog, allowing him to lick his hands.

The professor's mind wandered—he felt uneasy. He looked at the corpse and then at the fluffy little dog at his feet, who, after all, was part of God's creation.

'Like a man casts off old garments to put on new ones…so does the soul…'

No, no, he said to himself. He shouldn't allow such uncharitable thoughts to cross his mind. But he couldn't check his mind. It wasn't impossible. The Gita said so, too. And he bent down again and patted the pup with more tenderness and fellow feeling.

The procession was on the move. I was in front, uncomfortably laid within the glass hearse, with half a dozen people walking behind. It went down towards the river.

By the time it had passed the main street, I found myself in solitude. Some of the lawyers had left at the high court. My author friend had branched off to the coffee house, still smoking. At the local college, the professor gave me a last, longing, lingering look and sped up the slope to his classroom. The remaining six or seven disappeared into the district courts.

I began to feel a little small. Lesser men than myself had had larger crowds. Even a dead pauper carried on a municipal wheelbarrow got two sweepers to cart him off. I had only one human being, the driver, and even he seemed to be oblivious of the enormity of the soul whose decayed mansion he was transporting on its last voyage. As for the horse, he was positively rude.

The route to the cremation ground is marked with an infinite variety of offensive smells. The climax is reached when one has to branch off the main road towards the crematorium along a narrow path which runs beside the city's one and only sewer. It is a stream of dull, black fluid with bubbles bursting on its surface all the time.

Fortunately for me, I was given some time to ruminate over my miscalculated posthumous importance. The driver pulled up under a large peepal tree near where the road turns off to the cremation ground. Under this peepal tree is a tonga stand and a water trough for horses to drink out of. The horse made for the water and the driver clambered off his perch to ask the tonga drivers for a light for his cigarette.

The tonga drivers gathered round the hearse and peered in from all sides.

'Must be someone rich,' said one. 'But there is no one with him,' queried another. 'I suppose this is another English custom—no one goes to funerals.'

By now I was thoroughly fed up. There were three ways open to me. One was to take the route to the cremation ground and, like the others that went there, give myself up to scorching flames, perhaps to be born again into a better world, but probably to be extinguished into nothingness. There was another road which forked off to the right towards the city. There lived harlots and other people of ill-repute. They drank and gambled and fornicated. Theirs was a world of sensation and they crammed their lives with all the varieties which the senses were capable of registering. The third one was to take the way back. It was difficult to make up one's mind. In situations like these the toss of a coin frequently helps. So I decided to toss the coin; heads and I hazard the world beyond; tails and I go to join the throng of sensation seekers in the city; if it is neither heads nor tails and the coin stands on its edge, I retrace my steps to a humdrum existence bereft of the spirit of adventure and denuded of the lust for living.

AND TWO WHO FLATTERED TO DECEIVE

LAL KRISHNA ADVANI
(b. 1927)

My worry today is the rise of right-wing, fascist parties in the country. The youth of today should be aware of the rise in communal politics and the dangers involved. If we love our country, we have to save it from communal forces. And though the liberal class is shrinking, I do hope that the present generation totally rejects communal and fascist policies. I shun people who are at the forefront of this communalism, and this includes the likes of L. K. Advani.

When I had first met Advani, I thought he was forthright and clean and able. So we kept in touch. In 1989, he chose me to file his papers for nomination to Parliament, and I supported him by proposing his name as MP from New Delhi. I set my hopes on him because Sikhs were targeted by the Congress in 1984 and Advani seemed to be the only choice. Advani cashed in, and there were photos and banners and what not. But my disillusionment began when he started fouling the atmosphere of the country.

The one event that pitchforked Advani to centre stage and reshaped India's politics was his rath yatra from Somnath to Ayodhya, leading to the destruction of the Babri Masjid on 6 December 1992. He, more than anyone else, sensed that Islamophobia was deeply ingrained in the minds of millions of Hindus; it only needed a spark to set it ablaze. The choice of Somnath as the starting point and Ayodhya as the terminal one was well-calculated. Mahmud Ghazni had destroyed the temple at Somnath; Ayodhya was believed to be the birthplace of Sri Ram—it was bruited about that a temple to mark the birth site had stood there till Babur destroyed it and built a mosque over the ruins. This is disputed by historians and the matter was being pursued in law courts. Advani ignored legal niceties and arrived with great fanfare at the site. Since he was determined to build a new Ram temple at the same spot, the fate of the mosque was sealed. What happened there on that fateful day was seen on television by millions of people round the globe. And the repercussions were felt over the world. Hindu and Sikh temples were targeted by irate Muslims from Bangladesh to the UK. There were communal confrontations in different parts of India: the serial blasts in Bombay, the attack on the Sabarmati Express in Godhra, the massacre of innocent Muslims in Gujarat—they can all be traced back to the fall of the Babri Masjid. Relations between Hindus and Muslims have never been the same in India. However, the BJP reaped a rich harvest, won many of the elections that followed and eventually installed Atal Behari Vajpayee as prime minister and L.K. Advani as his deputy.

Advani claims that breaking the mosque was not on his agenda; that he actually sent Murli Manohar Joshi and Uma Bharati to plead with those who went on the rampage to desist. If that is so, why were the two seen embracing each other and rejoicing when the nefarious task was completed? We don't need the verdict of the Liberhan Commission to tell us what happened—we saw it with our own eyes. And, in his memoir, Advani recorded the jubilation that followed at the site, along with his triumphal return to Delhi. At an event at the IIC, I told Advani to his face, in front of an audience, 'You have sowed the seeds of communal disharmony in the country and we are paying the price for it.'

The one time Advani faltered in his steps was when he visited Karachi and praised Jinnah's speech to the Pakistan Constituent Assembly on 11 August 1947 as 'a classic exposition of a secular state'. It might well have been so, but Jinnah's speech was delivered at a time when millions of Hindus and Sikhs were being driven out of Pakistan or being slaughtered, and an equal number of Muslims were being driven out of India. It was a bloody exchange in which over a million died and over ten million were uprooted. Advani's eulogy must have pleased Pakistanis; it was badly received in India, particularly by his colleagues in the RSS and the BJP.

Advani should have left the political scene in a blaze of glory; but not many tears will be shed for him now. And for good reason. Did he ever regret the role he played in the demolition of the Babri Masjid? If he did, as he claims, why did he not tender an apology? Did he regret the anti-Muslim pogrom in Gujarat? If so, why did he protect Narendra Modi from being sacked as Prime Minister Vajpayee evidently wanted? It was a symbiotic relationship between the two—Modi helped Advani win elections from Gandhinagar; Advani, in turn, exonerated him from the anti-Muslim pogrom charges of 2002. Is it possible that as home minister Advani did not know of Jaswant Singh's mission to Kandahar to swap three jihadi militants for 150-odd Indians held hostage in hostile territory? There cannot be an iota of truth in his statement that he knew nothing about Jaswant's mission till it was over. Advani once described Manmohan Singh as 'nikamma'—useless. It so happens that Manmohan is still very much in use, whereas Advani's own erstwhile colleagues have pronounced him of no use any longer.

Advani has done grievous harm to our efforts to create a truly secular India. I have no regret over his discomfiture and eventual fadeout from national politics—it will be as comic a tragedy as any we have witnessed in recent times.

SANJAY GANDHI
(1946–1980)

I have been criticized and attacked more often than most people I know. It does not bother me; I ignore it all or laugh it off. The one criticism I have faced that I take seriously is to do with my support for Sanjay Gandhi. In 1975, after Mrs Gandhi declared an Emergency in the country, I ran a cover story in the Independence Day issue of the *Illustrated Weekly of India* on her second son and partner-in-politics, Sanjay. I called it 'The Man Who Gets Things Done'. I have never lived this down, but I stand by the story. I believed that Sanjay was what the country needed at the time—a man of action who would bring discipline public offices, crack down on smugglers, clean up our cities and, most important, take serious steps to control our explosive population growth. I believed that he was doing all those things and I supported him, perhaps blindly. Outside the moment, it is easy to see the full picture.

I met Sanjay in the mid-1970s, when he was already unpopular among intellectuals and many of my fellow liberals who saw him as an extra-constitutional power and a potential tyrant. When I met him, I found him to be reasonable and courteous. He was the one who had called the meeting. He wanted to talk to me about his Maruti car business and wanted me to write about it. I went with him to the factory site. I was disappointed; it looked like the workshop of a blacksmith, a lohar. He took me around the site in a prototype of the Maruti car, driving fast and talking about how important the project was. I was more impressed by his passion and enthusiasm than by the physical set-up. It was being said in those days that Haryana's chief minister, Bansi Lal, had given Sanjay land for free for his factory. I found these allegations to be false. Sanjay had paid a fair price. I wrote this in my story on Maruti. That was how our association began. We became friends.

Sanjay was good-looking. He had an eye for pretty girls, but the good sense not to get carried away. He was also a teetotaller, but not self-righteous. Always polite, Sanjay sought me out for company and advice. I was flattered. Our friendship was strengthened after his marriage to Maneka, whose family I knew. They made a handsome couple. I was past sixty then and, like many people reaching old age, I enjoyed the attention of young and spirited people.

Since I also had a good equation with Mrs Gandhi in those days, I was dubbed the Gandhis' chamcha, especially when I supported the Emergency. Even now, after all these years, I think the Emergency was necessary, because the Opposition had unleashed chaos and nothing in the country functioned. I had no idea then that it could be and would be misused and abused. Sanjay was always extremely courteous to me, so I found it hard to believe stories about his dictatorial ways. When I first got to know him, he really did seem like a committed man who was always true to his word. He had a conscience. And he was a doer, impatient to bring about changes. Maybe that was what made him dictatorial.

A year or so into the Emergency, he became very unpopular because of the forced nasbandi (sterilization) programme, censorship and arbitrary slum demolitions. It was bruited about that he had ordered bulldozers to demolish the jhuggis of innocent people, and that men had been pulled out of buses and cinema halls and forcibly sterilized. Many of these were wild rumours, but it is true that Sanjay and his thuggish friends—they more than he—were beginning to run the country like their fiefdom. Mrs Gandhi had come to depend heavily on her dynamic younger son and had almost handed over the reins of power to him. Nobody could understand the hold he had on her. She both loved and feared him. There is a story that Sanjay once slapped his mother at the dinner table, with outsiders present, and she took it quietly.

What Sanjay did, or was alleged to have done, during the Emergency had given him the image of a monster. He and Maneka came to see me in Bombay shortly after the Congress had been voted out of power, with Mrs Gandhi losing badly in her constituency. When they came to my apartment on Arthur Bunder Road, there were mobs in the streets baying for Sanjay's blood. I had to drive the couple to the airport at some risk.

I stood by the Gandhi family during their days in the doghouse, when they were being persecuted by the Janata Party government, many of whose leaders the Gandhis had persecuted during the Emergency. My family and friends were very critical of me, and I had to face a great deal of flak. I watched with some satisfaction as Mrs Gandhi and Sanjay fought back and won the elections of 1980. But the happiness was brief. On the morning of 23 June 1980, Sanjay crashed his two-seater plane on the southern ridge in Delhi. Both he and his co-pilot, Captain Subhash Saxena, were killed. After his tragic death, it was left to his older brother, Rajiv—with whom he had had very little interaction—to support a shattered Indira Gandhi. There is some truth in the belief that she was never quite herself after Sanjay's death.

I liked Sanjay. But I am certain that if he had lived, this country would not have been a democracy. There would have been order and much faster development, but no democracy. I have been asked if, in that case, I would still have supported him. I don't know. He would probably have got around me. He could be a real charmer. Besides, he was a friend, and he had been good to me. It was because of him that I was nominated to the Rajya Sabha. And it was he who called up K. K. Birla and told him to give me the editor's job at the *Hindustan Times*. He did not need to do that, but he did. He was loyal, and so was I.

ACKNOWLEDGEMENTS

Many of the essays that appear in this volume are versions of pieces that first appeared in *Yojana, New Delhi*, the *Hindustan Times, Tribune, Illustrated Weekly of India, Statesman* and *Times of India*, to name a few of the publications that Khushwant Singh contributed to. As the majority of the pieces were taken from typescripts in the possession of the author's estate, it has been difficult to accurately source the name of the publication in which the pieces first appeared. All the essays in the book have been used with permission from the author's estate. Every effort has been made to trace copyright holders and obtain permission to reproduce copyright material included in the book. In the event of any inadvertent omission, the publisher should be informed and formal acknowledgement will be included in all future editions of this book.